NEW TRADE SHOW DESIGN

New Trade Show Design / 新銳商業展會設計
Edition 2008

Author / Jacobo Krauel
作者 / Jacobo Krauel
Graphic design & production / Roberto Bottura, architect
圖像設計制作 / Roberto Bottura, architect
Collaborators / Oriol Vallés & Raquel Castro
合作者 / Oriol Vallés & Raquel Castro
Text edited & translated / Jay Noden
文字編輯翻譯 / Jay Noden

© Carles Broto i Comerma
© Designer Books

Publishers / Designer Books & Links
出版 / 迪賽納圖書 & Links
Distributors / Designer Books
圖書發行 / 迪賽納圖書
B-0619, No.2 Building, Dacheng International Center, 78 East 4th Ring Middle Road,
Chaoyang District, Beijing, China
Tel: 0086-10-5883-1335 (Beijing);   0086-22-2341-1250 (Tianjin);
     0086-21-5596-7639 (Shanghai);   0086-571-8884-8576 (Hangzhou);
     0086-25-5807-5096 (Nanjing);   0086-512-6727-5123 (Suzhou);
     0086-755-8825-0425 (Shenzhen);   0086-20-8756-5010 (Guangzhou);
     0086-28-8665-0016 (Chengdu);   0086-27-5951-0042 (Wuhan);
     0086-23-6772-5751 (Chongqing);
Fax: 0086-10-5962-6193
E-mail: info@designerbooks.com.cn
http: //www.designerbooks.com.cn

Printed in China

ISBN: 978-84-96424-76-0
定價: HK$298.00

NEW TRADE SHOW DESIGN

Index

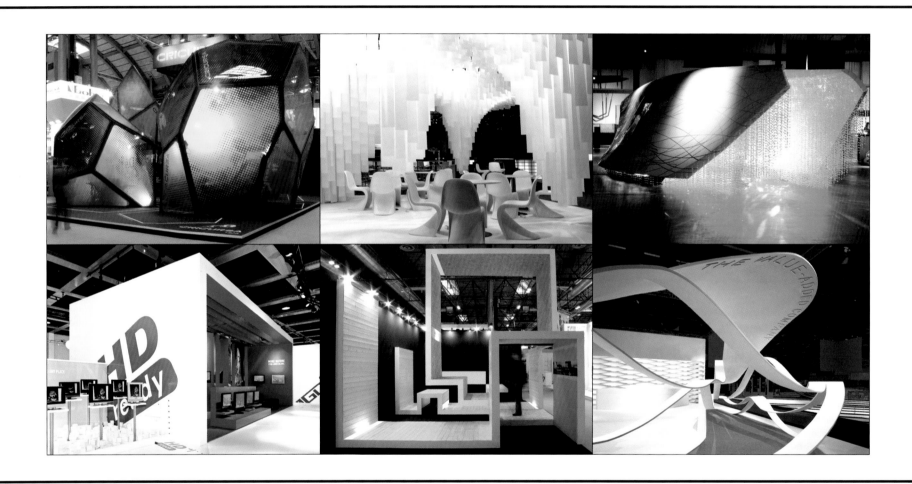

INTRODUCTION

In today's media-saturated and design-savy market place, a company's image is just as important to its success as the quality of the product service it provides. Top companies dedicate a considerable part of their resources to creating a strong corporate image that sets them apart from competitors. Increasingly, this includes developing a strong presence at industry trade fairs, which play an important role in attracting potential clients. This situation has led many companies to engage the services of some of the leading names in architecture and design when planning their stands, and to the birth of a new hybrid discipline combining cutting-edge elements of both marketing and spatial design. Designing a stand is a new kind of challenge for architects and designers. It requires them to transmit the essence of a company in a much smaller scale and time frame than traditional architecture, allowing them to experiment and propose unusual and innovative solutions. In order to be successful, a stand must balance a striking and eye-catching design with perfectly reflecting the company's products and image. The 50 stands in this collection have been selected according to this criteria. Some of the most innovative architectural work being done today is illustrated here, with designers using unusual materials and the latest technology to differentiate their designs and create a lasting impression in a short time. Ranging from modest one-room stalls to sprawling, multi-story stands and representing industries as diverse as jewerly, automobiles, construction materials and furniture, this collection surveys the spectrum of stand styles, from the simple and classy to high-tech or experimental designs. It includes the work of some of the most respected and brilliant professionals and design groups, such as Quinze & Milan, D'art Design and Coordination among others. We hope this overwiev of the most interesting work being done in this rapidly evolving fields will be a source of insight and inspiration for the reader.

Pentagram Design
Sonance

Cedia Expo 2007, Denver, Colorado, USA

Sonance offers innovative loudspeaker solutions that blend with upscale interiors. This exhibit marked the launch of Sonance's new graphic identity, as well as the first of a range of new architectural in-wall and ceiling speakers. Both the identity and the new products were also designed by Pentagram. The form of the exhibit therefore sought to three-dimensionally embody the spirit and language of these designs. It also had to anticipate the functional needs of a number of future smaller exhibit locations, and therefore had to be scaleable. The design solution was a series of abstract room sets, rising up to the maximum permitted height of 20 ft. Each provided counter, wall, ceiling and graphic display surfaces for Sonance's interior products. The Mariner outdoor speakers and a display for their sister company iPort, were placed around the Sets. All were supported by a large round information counter on the corner of the exhibits' primary and secondary aisles, as well as a number of freestanding interactive displays and two open conference and hospitality areas. The form of the room sets derived from a 3-dimensional interpretation of Sonance's new mark—a series of expanding squares suggestive of a growing volume of sound. Reconfig-ured as architectural forms, and left solid or hollowed out and filled with colored light, these squares – now cubes—could suggest a series of giant harmonic bullhorns. They were arranged linearly and skewed on plan for maximum visual effect when viewed from each of the four corners of the exhibit, and when visible from neighboring booths.

Design:
Pentagram Design

Photographs:
contributed by Padgett & Co.

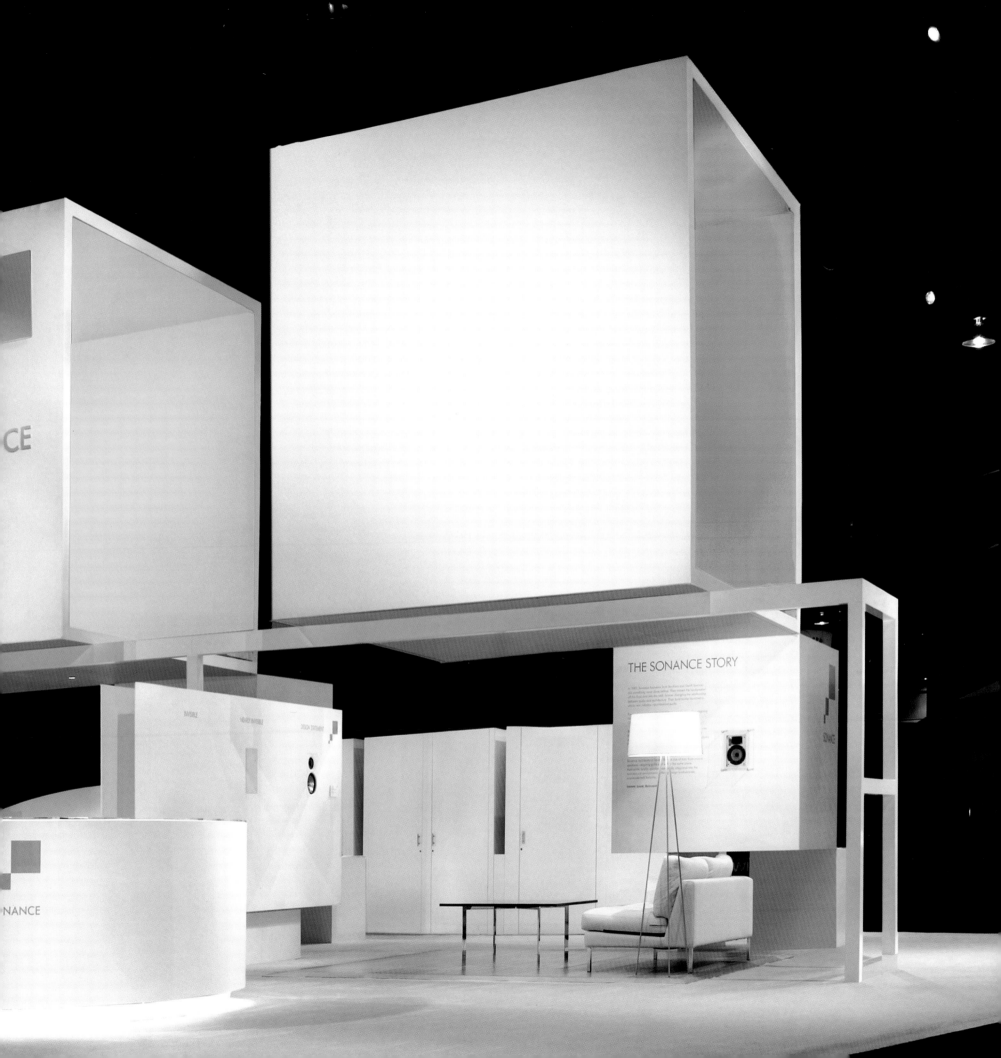

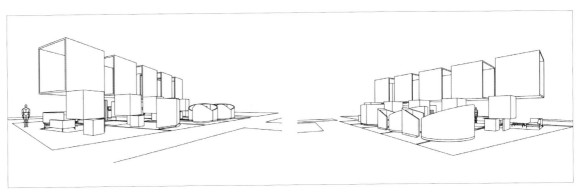

Zaha Hadid

Ideal House Cologne

IMM 2007, Cologne, Germany

Zaha Hadid Architects is particularly interested in bringing new typologies of living space to the forefront by creating an interpretation or manifestation of an ideal house. Ideal House Cologne was an excellent opportunity for the practice to experiment on a smaller, more temporal scale. This was a chance for them to test out ideas in a non-permanent environment and find out what works, and what needs fine-tuning.

Their design for Ideal House '07 was indicative of how this team of architects would like future living to be – a built manifesto that suggested an entirely new type of living environment. It was a re-invention of space, a latent environment whose morphology is not yet associated with familiar typologies or codes of conduct.

The front of the stand rises like the bows of a ship, the red exterior forming a sharp contrast with the white interior. The rooms here all seem to have been carved from a single block, leaving amorphous gaps, like caves, and there is not a straight line in sight. A red staircase, creating a link with the exterior, leads to a second floor where more rooms can be found. All the spaces here boast the irregular yet flowing shapes of the designer's furniture.

The stand represented a shift in thought process regarding the idea of the home, whereby people are beginning to see the importance of the environments they live in, in terms of the possibilities of how to make a space really work for them, both in the functional sense, but also the more intangible benefits of being grounded in a space that is aesthetically pleasing. The complete marriage of form and function was seen here as being crucial – one should never be sacrificed for the other.

Design:
Zaha Hadid
Patrik Schumacher

Photographs:
Koelnmesse

Project Architect:
Woody Yao

Design Team:
Melodie Leung,Eddie Can, Daniel Baerlecken, Muthahar Khan

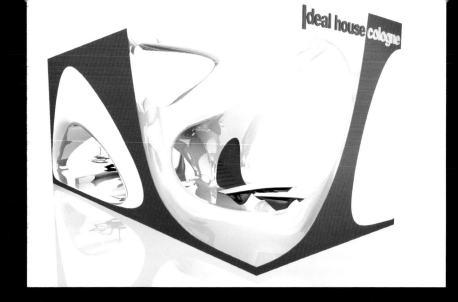

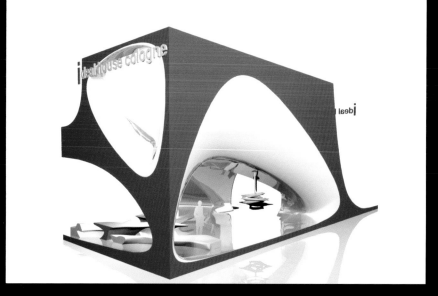

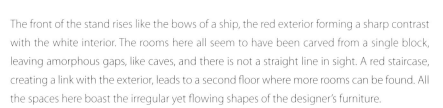

The front of the stand rises like the bows of a ship, the red exterior forming a sharp contrast with the white interior. The rooms here all seem to have been carved from a single block, leaving amorphous gaps, like caves, and there is not a straight line in sight. A red staircase, creating a link with the exterior, leads to a second floor where more rooms can be found. All the spaces here boast the irregular yet flowing shapes of the designer's furniture.

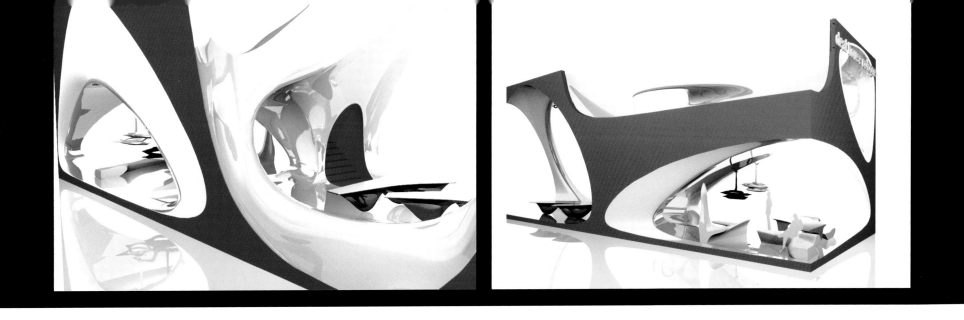

Quinze & Milan

Moroso - 'Caged Beauty'

Interior Biënnale 2006, Kortrijk, Belgium

Arne Quinze created the theme for the Moroso booth at Interieur Biënnale 2006, Belgium's biggest furniture fair, held in the town of Kortrijk. Over the years the designer has created a solid partnership with this prestigious company, who design and produce high-quality and luxurious sofas, armchairs and accessories.

The designer opted to afford the stand a high level of transparency and accessibility but at the same time to put each design on a pedestal in honor of their creators.

The result is this sculpture constructed from glass fiber cages, which keep all the beauty of the display pieces inside yet allow them to remain fully visible to the public. The blocks have been put together forming shelves, where items of furniture are on display, and defining different spaces on the floor plan. Decorative elements in the form of items of furniture hang from this versatile structure, thus creating a bizarrely incongruous optical effect with chairs apparently resting on a vertical surface. The splashes of color from the furniture are greatly enhanced thanks to the whiteness that surrounds them.

The aesthetic of this structure from the outside is an industrial one and from a distance the booth resembles a factory with towers projecting from different places.

Design & concept:
Arne Quinze

Photographs:
Thierry van Dort for Quinze & Milan

Construction:
Quinze & Milan

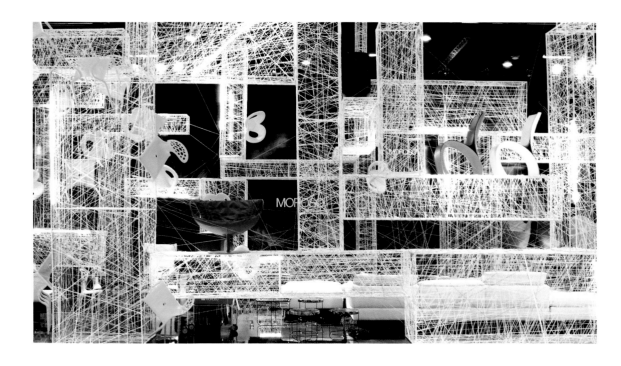

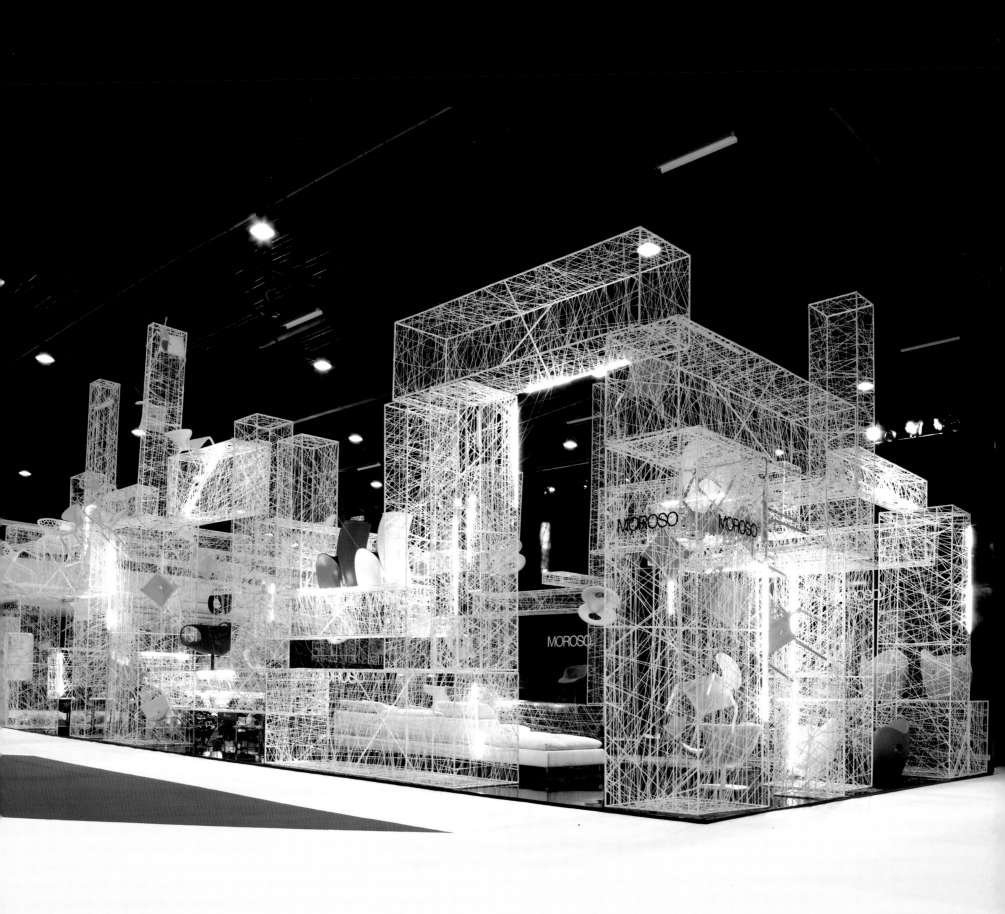

The designer opted to afford the stand a high level of transparency and accessibility but at the same time to put each design on a pedestal in honor of their creators.

The result is this sculpture constructed from glass fiber cages, which keep all the beauty of the display pieces inside yet allowing them to remain fully visible to the public.

The blocks have been put together forming shelves, where items of furniture are on display, and defining different spaces on the floor plan.

Decorative elements in the form of items of furniture hang from this versatile structure, thus creating a bizarrely incongruous optical effect with chairs apparently resting on a vertical surface.

Etón Corporation

Etón Corporation

CES 2007, Las Vegas, USA

Etón Corporation is an American based company that is famous for producing shortwave radios. Known for their innovative and stylish products, Etón had the incredible challenge of creating a booth for CES 2007, an international tradefair for electronic consumables. They needed to create something that would catch the eye, welcome visitors in and turn their focus from the booth to the products themselves. In addition to looking good, the booth also had to be extremely utilitarian to support nearly constant meetings throughout the day and the more than 20-person trade show staff.

The design theme was a dynamic, open sculpture. "The booth is basically a statement to 20 years of Etón and the dynamic change in the borderless radio medium that has been building momentum over the last decade and is sure to continue through the next", says Jesse Kearney, Director of Corporate Communications at Etón Corporation.

The whole booth concept, made of aluminum wrapped with a white spandex cloth created metal shapes arranged over the 40-by-60 foot exhibits' white laminate flooring. These bizarre shapes added a futuristic flavor to the exhibition reflecting Etón's dedication to researching and developing their products. Illuminating this white space were two more non-traditional shapes suspended via an aluminum truss 20 feet over the exhibit – a 22-foot "snake" and a 27-foot long "cloud". Fluorescent lights inside the surreal shapes lit up the floor below, where display stands made of acrylic and medium-density fiberboard featured the radios all designed by Etón. The range of radios on display formed a striking contrast to the white background creating the effect of highlighting the product. Furthermore, since white is the purest of all the colors it conveys and enhances a feeling of precision, which guests to the stand would associate with the company's technology. Orange chairs complement the colors found on the company logo and avoid the stand appearing excessively bland. The intention was to evoke the borderless nature of radio itself and of Etón's products, which enable people to enjoy this medium wherever they are in the world. The goal, according to Jesse Kearney, was to "trigger curiosity and to share our excitement for the new generation of technologies which our products are adopting".

Design:
Etón Corporation

Photographs:
H.G. Esch, Cologne

Creative Director:
Jesse Kearney, Eton Corporation,
Palo Alto, California

Booth Design:
Gunther Spitzley, Visionworks, Zurich

Design Team Etón:
Vania Kong, Philip Tsang, Binh Tran,
Etón Corporation, Palo Alto, California

Booth Builder:
Droste, Gelsenkirchen Germany

The range of radios on display formed a striking contrast to the white background creating the effect of highlighting the product. Furthermore, since white is the purest of all the colors it conveys and enhances a feeling of precision, which guests to the stand would associate with the company's technology. Orange chairs complement the colors found on the company logo and avoid the stand appearing excessively bland.

The intention was to evoke the borderless nature of radio itself and of Etón's products, which enable people to enjoy this medium wherever they are in the world. The goal, according to Jesse Kearney, was to "trigger curiosity and to share our excitement for the new generation of technologies which our products are adopting".

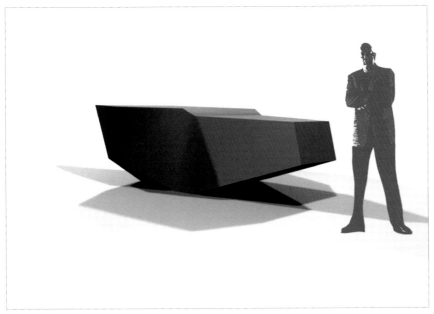

Schmidhuber + Partner

Audi

IAA, 2007, Frankfurt, Germany

Audi is presented at the 2007 IAA in a stand with streets that organize the vehicle exhibition and the flow of visitors. This language of curves is developed along the entire exhibit and completely surrounds the fair stand. The curves penetrate the outward facing buildings and produce diagonal openings and lines of sight, creating a type of urban market. Upon entering the stand, the fair visitors are immediately submerged in the world of Audi.

A wide opening in one of its sides takes you to the catwalk; a bright, white path on the floor and ceiling that accompanies the visitor and leads him all the way through the product displays until arriving at a large step that ends at a higher level. The stand can be enjoyed in its entirety from this point of view.

The catwalk is the most outstanding element and main means of communication with the newcomer at the IAA: the Audi A4. You can get to know all the aspects of its innovative design and the new technology used in this model with the interactive stations. The path leads up to grandstand with steps so that the visitors can pause, sit and observe the stage designed for the Audi A4 and conceived to focus all attention on it. Finally, a space is reached through the informative path where the vehicle is accessible. At the end of the catwalk there is the closed off and exclusive "A4 lounge". It completely reflects the new image of the vehicle with its innovative design and new quality technology that one would find in the best limousines. Everything inside is adapted to the vehicle; the car seems to navigate in a dark room as if it were driving through an aerodynamic tunnel. The quality and dynamic of the new A4 is experienced in an exclusive, almost private environment.

Some materials are withheld to reserve the spotlight for the colours of the car so that they appear more vibrant. The physical architecture is expressed in nuances between matte and shiny white. The shiny highlights are expressly included within the stand so that the more important spaces stand out thanks to the play on contrast. Here the surfaces change room matte to brilliant, from white to black. The architectural dynamic is enforced through this contrast and the elements of white furniture seem to float above the black floor.

Design:
Concept and architecture by
Schmidhuber + Partner, Munich

Concept and communication by
Mutabor Design, Hamburg

Photographs:
Andreas Keller, Altdorf

Client:
AUDI, Ingolstadt

Lighting:
Four to One: scale design, Hürth

Telecommunication installation:
NIYU media projects, Hocke & Hofmann GbR, Berlin

Climate control installation:
Hartmut Meyer GmbH, Krefeld

Structural engineers:
RPB Rückert GmbH, Heilbronn

Collaborators:

Assembly:
Messebau Tünnissen, Kranenburg

Audiovisual assembly:
AG, Köln

Graphic production:
GmbH, Düsseldorf

Lighting equipment:
Showtec Lichtechnik, Köln

Metalwork:
Syscon, Sys.constr., Hockenheim

Area:
3900 sqm groundfloor
1600 sqm first floor

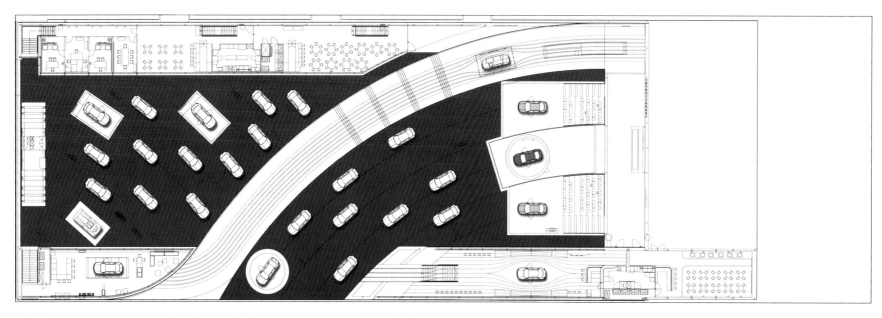

Peter Schmidt Group

Wöhner

Hanover trade fair 2007, Germany

The Wöhner company is a global leader in bus bar system technology. The brand identity and the corporate design, both developed by the Peter Schmidt Group, made their first appearance at the Hanover Trade Fair 2007, where they were transported into a third dimension. The corporate design and brand space of the company were brought together within a single space. Through its architecture, the stand boasts Wöhner's core competences in both modularity and scaling ability, highlighting their system technology. The technology of modularity ensures that the construction system appears highly compatible and extremely variable, while the scaling ability works with the principle of adaptability, so that the trade fair stand can be aligned seamlessly to new conditions time and again. As a result both technologies facilitate totally individual and flexible use.

In keeping with Wöhner's advertising slogan: "Everything with voltage" the composition language together with the direction of light and color relate to each other in ways which are both diverse and innovative. The result is the development of a dialogue between the different elements. The basic parts that form this composition and the colors in general are played down throughout and their simplicity lends special emphasis and focus on what is essential. The stand conveys timelessness through the use of white and silvery-gray, while the use of fluorescent orange corresponds with Wöhner's policy to annually change their identity recognition colors, which are also used in the company and brand communications, e.g. in brochures and catalogues. Both the colors used as well as the "typo carpet" formed by the repetition of the phrase: "Everything with voltage" are therefore identical.

The trade fair stand has successfully been transformed into a venue largely thanks to the curtain of light that floats above the entire space. The changing colors together with the surprising range in tones act as a beacon and allow the Wöhner brand to be clearly visible at a distance. The lounge area forms the centerpiece and is clearly separated from areas in the inner room. It serves as a place of retreat and provides the opportunity for informal discussions. On the other hand in the variable meeting cubicles on both sides the privacy screen provides protection from interruption.

Everything is directed at the individual visitor, who is invited to attend, obtain information and hold discussions, to discover new ideas and, simply, just to stay a while and relax.

Design:
Peter Schmidt Group

Leading architect:
Amir Rezaii

Photographs:
Jörg Hempel

bachmann.kern & partner

Siegwerk Druckfarben AG

Drupa 2004, Düsseldorf, Germany

Design:
bachmann.kern & partner

Photographs:
contributed by bachmann.kern & partner

Siegwerk Group International is a world-leading independent ink manufacturer with a long history, dating back to 1830. The company has established a reputation of reliability, innovative solutions, high quality and teamwork.

Siegwerk's stand was one of the more prominent spaces at drupa 2004, a trade fair for the printing and paper industries that takes place every 4 years in Düsseldorf, Germany. The primary aim for the printing company was to improve customer relations through the presentation of their product and their achievements. Other important aspects were their new business strategies and Siegwerk's publicity campaign.

The challenge for Siegwerk's presentation at the fair, in terms of the booth dimensions, its effect when seen from a distance and the open design was to create a concept that visualized the company's attributes. The final stand was a perfect reflection Siegwerk's qualities. The red cube communicated consistency, technological know-how and high quality products, while the glowing wave demonstrated the company's flexibility and dynamism, as well as symbolizing the printing process.

The stand focused on communication and information. In the wave area the visitors could find out more about the company with the help of information displays, leaflets and multimedia presentations. Chairs and bar tables were arranged in four areas of the booth for seeing potential clients. The information desk was positioned in the entrance to the two-story red cube and all visitors were welcomed in and escorted into the bistro area located on the ground floor. This space gave visitors a chance to talk in a quieter, more relaxed environment.

A desk was placed in front of the staircase, which led to the upper floor, where the VIP and meeting rooms were located. Reservations for the two VIP rooms and the five meeting rooms could be made here. In addition to these rooms the upper floor included the kitchen with an elevator for food and drinks and the office with storage.

Red netting enclosed the cube allowing people to see into the bistro area from outside of the booth. Upstairs the meeting rooms required sound proofing, so the architects erected glass panels behind the netting.

Bachmann kern & partner were also responsible for designing products related to the stand such as a flip-book containing images of the stand, which was handed out to visitors, and a calendar for company employees, which documented the development of the stand during the 90 days leading up to the start of the fair.

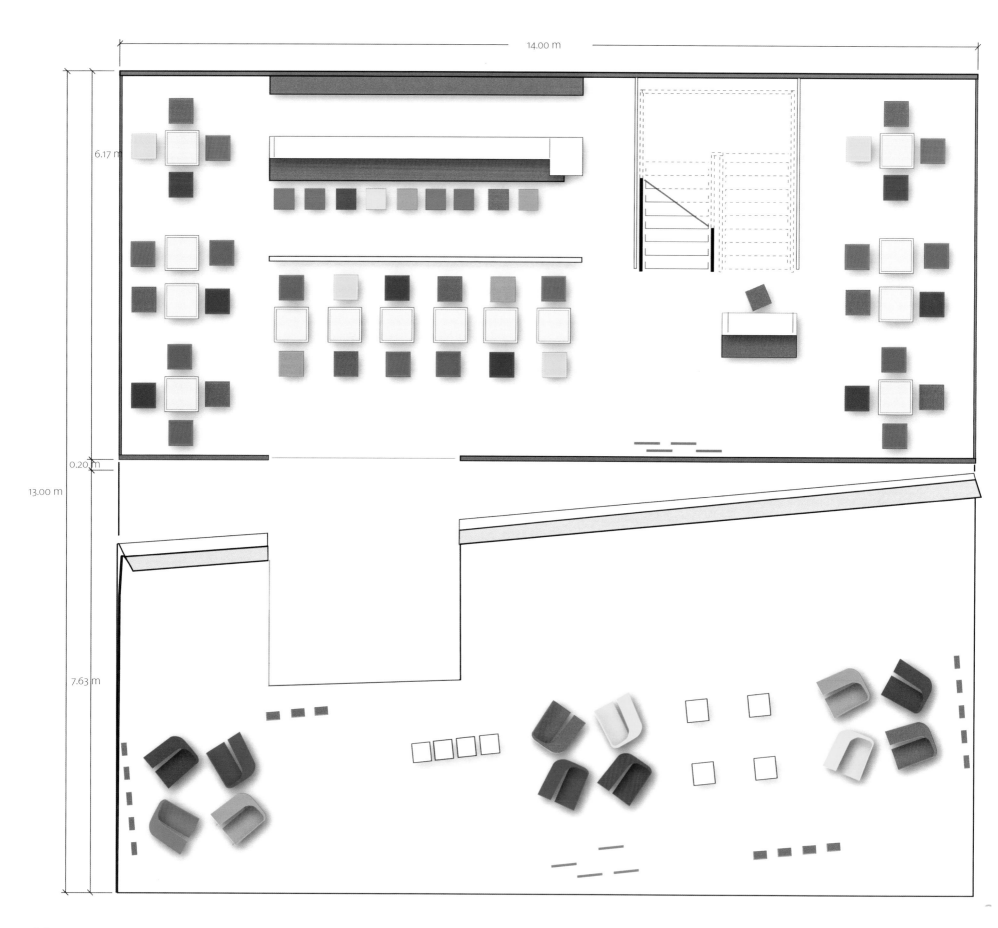

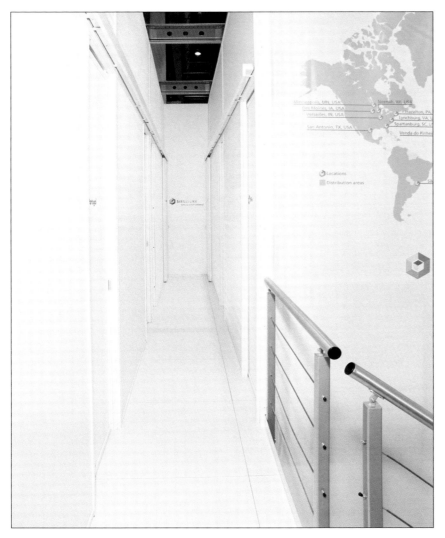

A desk was placed in front of the staircase, which led to the upper floor, where the VIP and meeting rooms were located. Reservations for the two VIP rooms and the five meeting rooms could be made here. In addition to these rooms the upper floor included the kitchen with an elevator for food and drinks and the office with storage.

Red netting enclosed the cube allowing people to see into the bistro area from outside of the booth. Upstairs the meeting rooms required sound proofing, so the architects erected glass panels behind the netting.

spek DESIGN

Gerriets Theater Equipment

Showtec 2007, Berlin, Germany

Until now, all of Gerriet's stands have had similar styles. They were stands with completely open showroom floors. This time, influenced by the company's new products a new stand concept had to be created to make use of the new generation G2-Frame controls, the Kabuki G2 drop reveal system and the new ShowLED animated curtain, etc.

To be able to offer the different sections of Gerriets' products a determined mood and showroom floor, the stand was divided into six zones: one for theatre curtains, shows and other events, another for the new G-FRAME controllers and the Kabuki G2 system, a technology and propulsion track zone, one for projection screens joined with the control room, a reception and information area, and finally the "Gerriets Café-Theatre", where the ShowLED curtain is displayed. Rooms one through four were occupied by the textile section with "stage foliage". This "foliage", white on the outside and black inside, hardly allowed one to see outside while, inside the rooms, offered a pleasant transparency. Thanks to this, the rooms obtained a wider and diaphanous ambience. The v-shaped central hallway that is found between the rooms opened to the café-theatre and shaped an accented focus towards the old chandeliers and the impressive ShowLED animated curtain. Both entrances to the stand allowed for an impressive view of the entire stand and "Café-Theatre Gerriets" offered a relaxed atmosphere for conversation while having a snack. The stage design obtained an artistic and pleasing environment so that the guests could relax, and at the same time served as a reception area for the visitors who specialised in the theatre sector.

The materials used were fabric for the walls, Gerriets "stage foliage" in black and white, and Gerriets "Expo" in black for the floor panelling. For the counters, bases of display objects and doors, panels of DM in black were used. And for the walls of the café, Gerriets cotton fabric was hung.

The stand contained a total of two independent surfaces with an exterior hallway leading to both, united by a continuous floor panelling, thanks to which, a wider effect was achieved in the stand. This way the exterior hallway could be used perfectly as a walkway area for the stand. The total surface area was 157 m2 (1670 ft2).

Thanks to the use of the client's own materials and self-production the stand was completed with a budget of 50,000€ ($74,250, £37,700). The stand was awarded the bronze Adam Award.

The new hardware for the G-FRAME controller by Gerriets, also designed by Spek Design and presented at the fair stand, was awarded the 2007 Showtech Award, as well as the silver 2007 Baden Württemberg Focus Safety International Prize for Design.

Design:
spek DESIGN
Nadine Molter, Alfe Toussaint,
Sandra Eßwein Patrick Sauter

Photographs:
Norbert Hordan and spek DESIGN

Graphic Design:
spek Design

Assembly:
Gerriets GmbH

Fabrics:
Gerriets GmbH

Lighting:
MegaForce

Area:
157 sqm (1670 sqft)

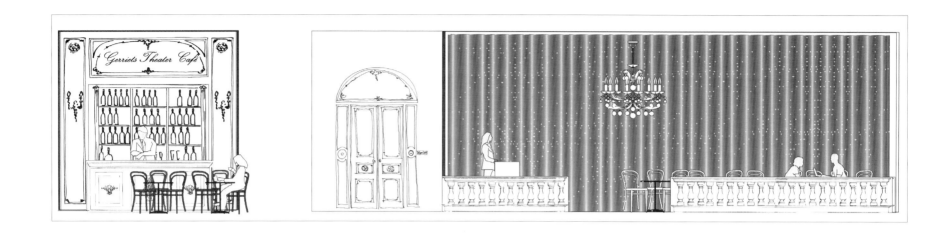

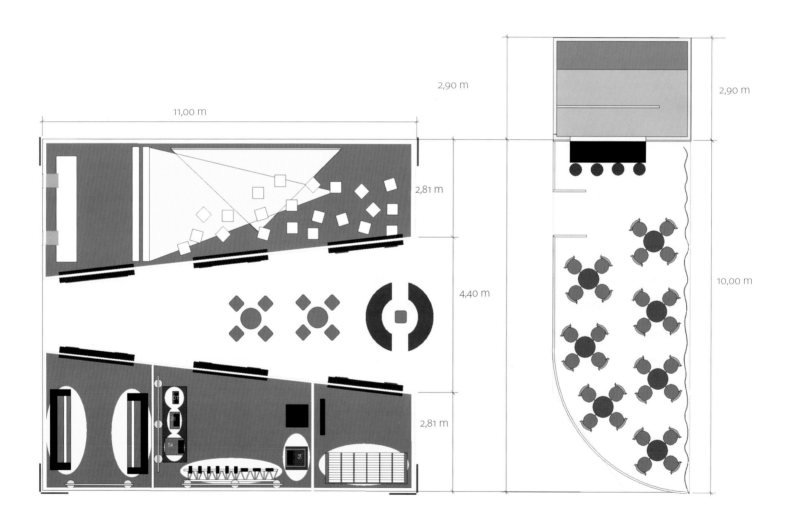

D'Art Design Gruppe

Philips Lighting

Light & Building 2006, Frankfurt, Germany

As the world's most important lighting trade fair, the biggest Light & Building exhibition venue put the entire market on display. More than 900 manufacturers presented lighting technology and lamps, decorative lighting fixtures and lighting components, in 80,000 sqm (860,215 sqft) of exhibition space.

Royal Philips Electronics is one of the biggest electronics companies in the world. It is the world leader in lighting, electric shavers, televisions, etc and has over 128,000 employees working in more than 60 countries.

In Light & Building 2006 the PHILIPS Licht business sector, a division of Royal Philips Electronics products, participated with its lighting sector.

The main idea revolved around the slogan "sense and simplicity": All superfluous details were eliminated. The deliberate reduction of colour and language of purist forms reinforced this impression. Throughout the entire space of the stand, different light zones were created, dedicated to a variety of themes, showing diverse scenes and settings with lighting applications for and with the person. Human figures explained in short phrases how light enriched their lives at the same time as the visitors were presented with the best solution and possibilities of application for the products exhibited in each of these light zones. "Home sweet home", for example, showed them the possibility of changing the colour of the rooms at their fancy using light. The room could be transformed using different types of light, giving it the ambient desired at any particular time, and without having to resort to a single paint brush! In this way, they made visitors aware of the different possibilities of light applications of the lamps and the settings which could be created in a realistic context.

With Philips being the main sponsor of the World Cup, this theme was not left out at the stand. Scenes of various football stadiums lit by Philips, along with the sound of thousands of fans cheering on their team, evoked the visitors' enthusiasm. After all the interaction, both experts and laymen were able to enjoy themselves in the Light & Wellbeing zone and discover what happens when light wins over tiredness. The Philips Lighting 2006 presentation turned out to be a truly sensorial and visual experience.

Design:
D'Art Design Gruppe

Photographs:
contributed by D'Art Design Gruppe

Area:
approx. 900 sqm

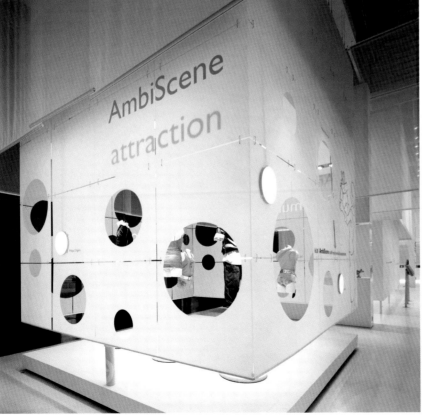

When visitors stepped into the stand, their eyes would immediately relax and any agitation would disappear. The clear architectural structure brought a sense of unity to a space which had constant new experiences prepared for visitors.

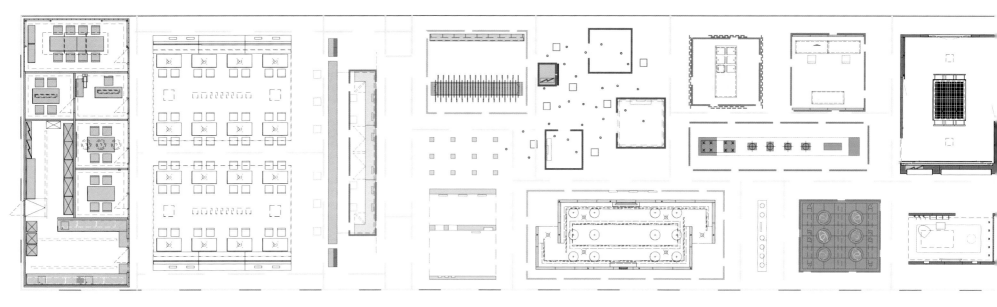

The design was based on creating different spaces which would generate a variety of experiences for the senses, using light as the basic element. Awaiting visitors was a world which considered light as the number one factor affecting the senses and visual experiences. The important feature was not so much the technical characteristics of the lights as their effect on and for people's lives.

The challenge faced when planning the distribution of the stand consisted of creating a display which covered the wide range of existing products and areas of application. The objective was to strengthen the company and the Philips brand, accentuating its position as world leader and its strong emphasis on innovation.

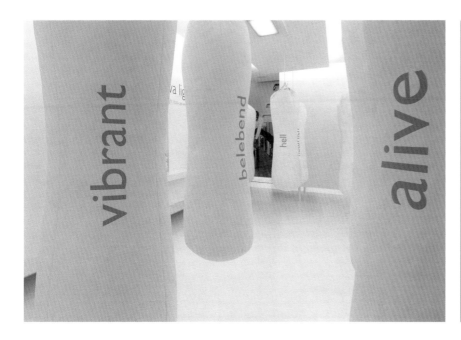

Emilio Pemjean Muñoz

Paislant

Construtec 2006, Madrid, Spain

With the aim of establishing work relations between architects as quality stand designers and exhibiting companies in search of new ways of presenting their products, CONSTRUTEC organized a competition in the construction hall for the design and construction of stands.

This stand is the result of the competition, projected and built by the company Aislamientos Pais.

"build a space with the materials on display"

The exhibitor manufactures insulating panels with a range of different finishes. Laminates were put together with the selected material and then folded allowing their exhibition in a position they could have when forming part of a building.

The stand modifies their perception from a more volumetric, frontal vision right down to the lateral fold, while at the same time the sequence of folded sides form spaces that float within a neutral and protective trihedron against an aggressive and uncontrolled environment.

The stand thereby establishes how each laminate should be, what needs to be considered, what happens in each and what shape they correspond to. Spaces have been created, places where visitors can come into direct contact with the materials and the forms that contain them, and where relationships can be established between visitors and exhibitors.

Design:
Emilio Pemjean Muñoz
Photography:
Emilio Pemjean Muñoz
Collaborator:
Jimena González Fejér

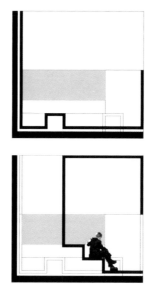

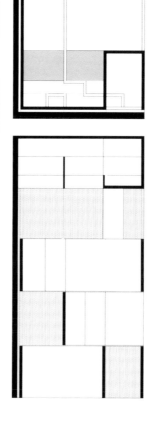

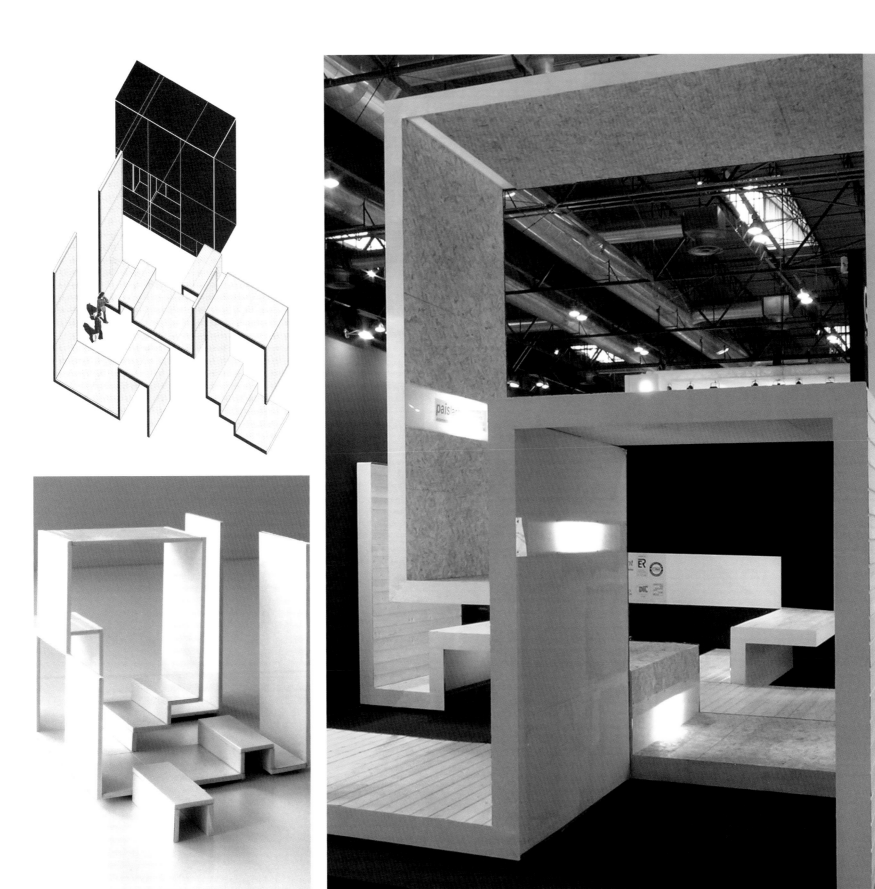

D'Art Design Gruppe

Gabor Shoes AG

GDS 2007, Düsseldorf, Germany

Shoemaker brand Gabor Shoes AG attends the international GDS shoe fair with a contrast-filled presentation, designed by D'Art Design Gruppe, establishing the new Gabor image on the international scene.

Since its foundation in 1949, the Gabor Shoes AG family brand has gone from being a traditional shoemaker to a worldwide leader in the shoe market making a name for itself as a lifestyle brand. This particular evolution has influenced the new design made by D'Art Design Gruppe.

The Gabor Shoes AG stand at the fair measures 780 sqm (8,387 sqft), clearly showing the brand's leadership in the market. The strong architecture is especially big on contrasts and keeps a balance between "simplicity" and "strength". For example, a rigid grid structure contrasts with a semitransparent elastic wall made of inflatable pads. This contrast symbolizes tradition and modernity as well as the prestigious shoemaker's strength in business and innovation.

The distinct exhibition points that are highlighted at the stand increase its transparency giving it the sensation of freedom provided by an open space, in which Gabor's essential products, like the Lifestyle Serie, Store Concept or Kids Corner, are presented in a significant manner.

Design:
D'Art Design Gruppe
Photographs:
contributed by D'Art Design Gruppe
Area:
780 sqm

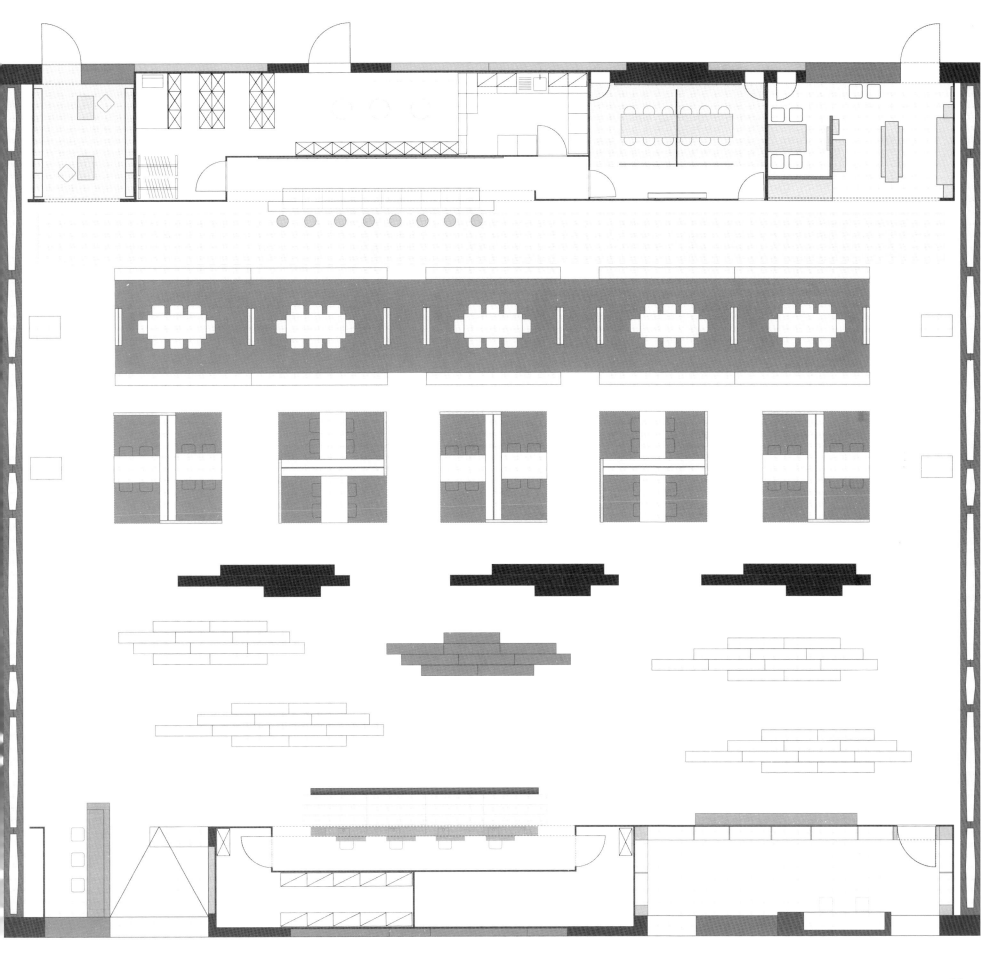

Braun Wagner

smart

International Motor Show 2007, Frankfurt, Germany

At the 2007 International Motor Show in Frankfurt smart once again set new standards regarding design, originality and dialogue with target groups. The brand presented itself with a striking, self-confident urban lifestyle concept. The installation was spread over various areas and consisted of the main brand presentation, smart History and a meeting area.

Like shop windows, meandering glass façades in the main presentation area generated space without creating rooms. They divided the stand into product presentation, an active area and a mall. The stand's message was 'spectacular and a novel'. In keeping with this brief the new smart fortwo was presented on a glass truss while body parts were presented in boutique-style within a glass case under the cars. The color and textile range of the smart interior was shown in the form of a slide-rule.

A back wall connected the three different stand areas and was used for diverse multimedia applications. At an interactive spray wall in the active area visitors were invited to participate in the creation of the smart city. They could create street art and send their personal digital graffiti as an e-card or download it on the Internet. On a LED screen, whose dynamic form matched the furniture, image and brand movies were shown that document smart's dedication to ecological issues.

The smart mall was integrated directly into the back wall as a meandering belt. The architectural language of the glass walls was repeated here. The smart core topic "safety" was displayed as an uplifted tridion safety cell and multi-media application. An airwall, lit from the inside, was integrated into the back wall transmitting the topic as a visual metaphor.

Core messages were integrated in an exposed, striking typography that matched the architecture. The catchwords "example", "dialogue", "independence" and "awareness" were fixed to the glass façades as apparently floating illuminated typography. The typographic concept symbolized a lively urban image.

A mirrored passage led from the presentation area to the smart History. The floor was covered with light fader plates where footprints remain visible for a couple of seconds, symbolizing the topics "sustainability" and "show the way". At smart History, bars were integrated into the ceiling to symbolize the bridging of the different smart eras. Multi-media and print communication as well as original model studies told the smart history.

The meeting area was a large space offering visitors a chance to relax. Large windows flooded the space with natural light, which is often missing in exhibition spaces.

Design:
Braun Wagner

Photographs:
Andreas Keller

Realisation stand:
Klartext

Realisation multi-media:
mu:d

Media production:
ms&p

Light planning:
Trussco

Realisation light:
Lightcompany

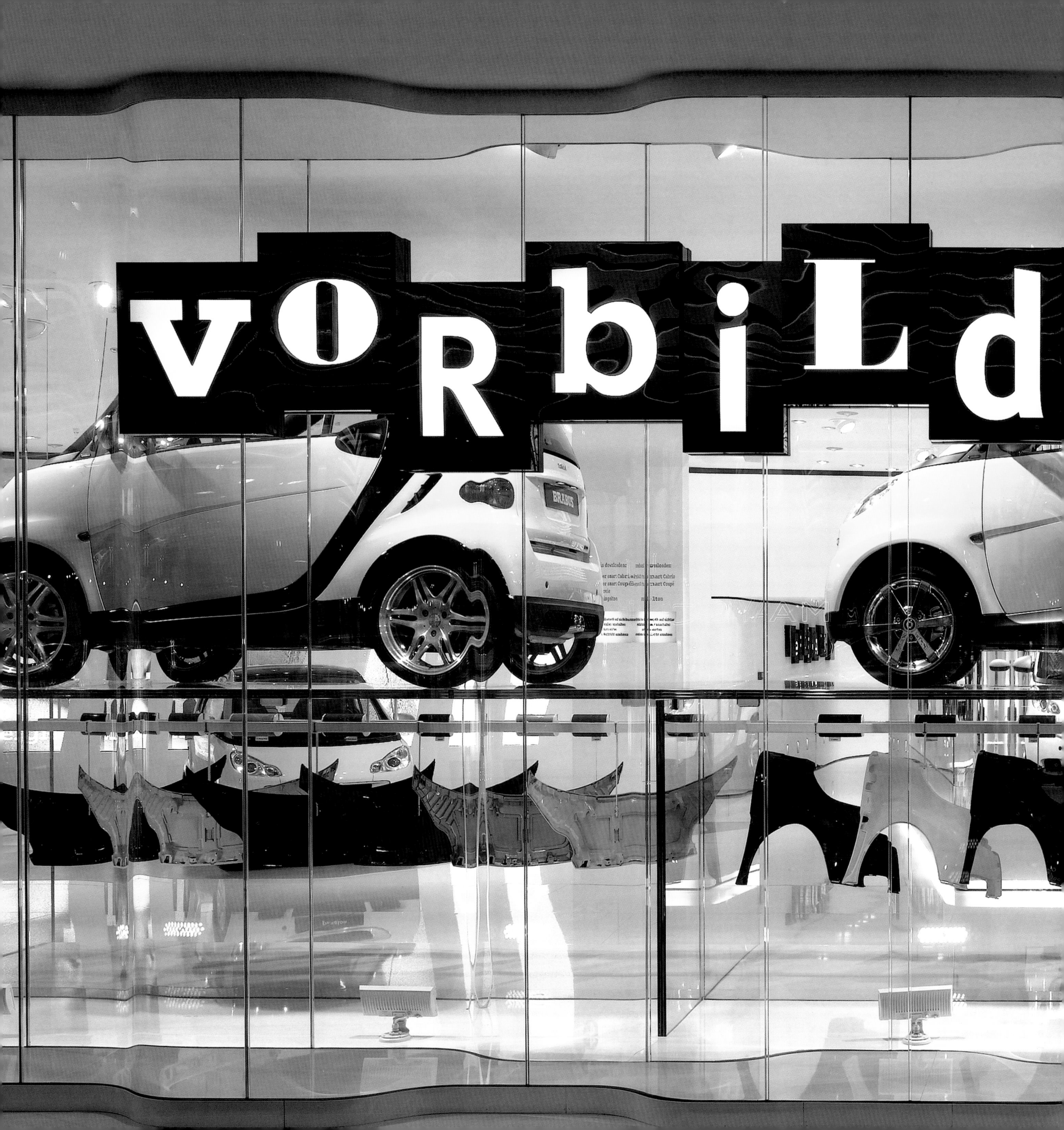
vORbiLd
BRABUS

The new smart mhd (Micro Hybrid Drive) was presented as a highlight on a platform that simulated the start/stop technology by way of a suspended LED cube that consisted of 3750 colour-changing LED balls.

>> Blau Metallic

>> Kristallweiß

>> Tiefschwarz

>> Rot Metallic

>> Silber Metallic

The stand's message was 'spectacular and novel'. In keeping with this brief the new smart fortwo was presented on a glass truss while body parts were presented in boutique-style within a glass case under the cars. The color and textile range of the smart interior was shown in the form of a slide-rule.

The meeting area was a large space offering visitors a chance to relax. Large windows flooded the space with natural light, which is often missing in exhibition spaces.

Grant Design Collaborative

Muzak

Global Shop 2005, Atlanta, Georgia, USA

Muzak holdings is a company best known for distributing music to retail stores and other companies. For GlobalShop, a major retail trade show in Las Vegas, Muzak wanted to promote its ability to accurately portray brands through sound, so the company turned to Atlanta based Grant Design Collaborative to design its 9 x 12 m (30 x 40 ft) exhibition space.

From the outside the booth appeared as a black box with semi-transparent curtains, which offered access on all four sides and enticed passers-by into finding out what was hidden inside. Each day the stand reinterpreted a different inanimate object: a red rose, a martini with a twist, and an eight ball. Each object was displayed repeatedly about a central cylinder giving them a 'wallpaper' effect. Music and scents were incorporated to complete the thematic and sensual experience. Grant Design Collaborative's strategic design showcased Muzak's ability to coordinate sound with brand and encouraged attendees to visit the booth more than once.

Overall, the space had a minimalist, lounge feel that encouraged potential customers to linger and experience Muzak's audio architecture capabilities for brands. Stools, chairs and tables gave visitors to the stand an opportunity to relax and reflect on the display.

Design:
Grant Design Collaborative
Photographs:
contributed by Grand Design Collaborative

The exhibit's circular core, adorned with the themed "prop of the day," and separated from the rest of the stand by a semi-transparent curtain, was created as a private meeting area for potential brand clients and Muzak's audio architects.

Walbert-Schmitz

Bayer MaterialScience

K2007, Düsseldorf, Germany

This stand was conceived by Walbert Schmitz and showcased at the K2007, one of the world's largest trade fair for the plastics industry. It combines the present with the future, concepts that form part of Bayer's corporate image, all of which floats in a sea of blue and green. The Bayer MaterialScience World was created on the basis of the Bayer logo colors. It was presented in an architectural design that portrayed it authentically and excitingly and created a structure that combined both reality and vision. The architecture, which was transparent, yet powerful, transformed the stand into a stage for the museum presentation of the exhibits. VisionWorks Today was bathed in blue and contained objects that are already part of everyday life today. VisionWorks Tomorrow, in green light, showed studies and visions for life tomorrow. Transparent ceiling constructions across exhibition areas with the same format provided a visual feeling of space. Molecular ScienceLights were to be viewed as a visible, symbolic link between plastic and finished product.

The processing of Bayer plastics within the stand itself, e.g. the cubes made from deep-drawing dies or the transparent rear wall in the lounge area, was a perfect complement to the presentation of a visionary philosophy and symbolized the flexible use of their own products.

The fair and stand constructors, demonstrated a keen understanding of these multidimensional requirements and presented Bayer MaterialScience at the fair with a high degree of conceptual and executive competence.

Design:
Walbert - Schmitz / BMS Communication Exhbition & Event
Photographs:
contributed by Walbert-Schmitz
Concept:
Heike Karsch for Walbert Schmitz
Area:
1342 sqm

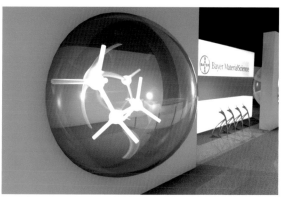

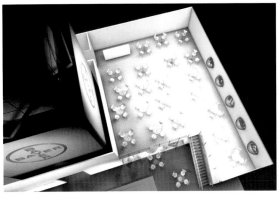

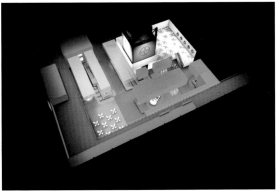

Demirden Design

Kutahya

Tüyap Fair and Congress, 2007, Istambul, Turkey

The aesthetical narration of the stand was mainly based on the dignified and sincere presentation of values like elegancy, romanticism and glory. The idea here was also to create a feeling of relaxation, a place where people could get away from the hustle and bustle of the rest of the exhibition.

The stand's whiteness wrapped around the guests with its swan-like pureness. The huge, high-ceilinged main structure acted as a gallery with its equivalent cylindrical forms. The white velvet fabric and tulles that reached from the ceiling to floor, measuring a height of 5.5 m (18 ft), identified the exhibiting spaces while also specializing them. Inside these spaces, bathroom scenes were set up in order to show the tiles in context. The displays could be made out from outside of the cylinders but visitors had to enter to truly appreciate them.

A seating area next to the stand clearly separated the act of looking at the product and relaxing to that of contemplating the selection. Visitors were therefore required to do one or the other and not both at the same time, thereby bringing a greater intensity to the two experiences.

The stand took on a timeless style through the use of the elegant, white columns, which seemed to come neither from the past nor the future. The columns had lights inside them allowing them to function both as support for the ceiling and as illumination. The space was therefore allowed to be highly minimalist, displaying the product and nothing more.

Design:
Demirden Design

Photographs:
Emre Ogan

Yeni bir dünyaya

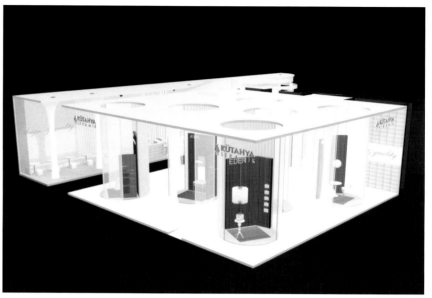

The stand's whiteness wrapped around the guests with its swan-like pureness. The huge, high-ceilinged main structure acted as a gallery with its equivalent cylindrical forms. The white velvet fabric and tulles that reached from the ceiling to floor, measuring a height of 5.5 m (18 ft), identified the exhibiting spaces while also specializing them. Inside these spaces, bathroom scenes were set up in order to show the tiles in context. The displays could be made out from outside of the cylinders but visitors had to enter to truly appreciate them.

Schmidhuber + Partner

O₂

CeBIT 2007, Hannover, Germany

The intention of O2's stand at the international CeBIT 2007 trade fair for computer technology was to present itself for the first time as a fully integrated one-stop telecommunications provider. The company sought to demonstrate their advance in the sector, which now offers the full range of communications solutions in the fixed network and in mobile telephony. This recent development was reflected in the location of their stand, directly neighboring Germany's largest telecommunications company, Deutsche Telekom.

The tradeshow exhibit gives the impression of being a modern café bar, thus emphasizing O2 Germany's image as a provider of high-quality service. The café bar provides a calm and pleasant atmosphere and invites visitors to retreat from the tradeshow bustle to discuss what they have seen and find out more, at their own unhurried pace, about what O2 Germany has to offer.

The varying tube lengths and spacing create distinct colorized pixels that merged into waves of images, giving visitors the impression of moving beneath a three dimensional "Media Cloud" with images wafting across it.

As a whole, the exhibit forms a cohesive brand world, which is clearly set apart from its tradeshow environment, simultaneously stimulating and relaxing visitors to the stand.

Design:
Concept and architecture by
Schmidhuber + Partner, Munich

Concept and communication by
KMS Team GmbH, Munich

Photographs:
Wolfgang Oberle, Munich

Client:
O2 Germany, Munich

Statics:
Posselt Consult, Übersee

Lighting:
Delux AG, Zürich

Media planning:
In Scena, Berlin

Radio planning:
phocus direct communication GmbH, Nürnberg

Realisation:
Messebau Tünnissen, Kranenburg

Light technic:
Limelight Veranstaltungstechnik GmbH, Gilching

Media:
Mixed Pixels

Media animation:
Jangled nerves, Stuttgart

Soundtechnician:
Neumann & Müller, München

Graphic products:
Schüttenberg, Düsseldorf

Area:
Ground floor
1635 sqm
First floor
506 sqm
Adjoining building
415 sqm

The new products are all presented in the interior of the exhibition stand. The booth is enclosed by a completely mirrored band, which multiplies the blue color of the "media cloud" ceiling structure increasing the sense of size in the space. This feature, which is already familiar from previous years, consists of Versa® PIXELs placed at the end of plastic tubes suspended from the ceiling.

Narcís Font & Cristian Vivas

FDModa

Bread & Butter, 2006, Barcelona, Spain

Narcis Font was asked to construct a stand for Bread & Butter, the fashion trade show that takes place in Barcelona. This is a trade show for creators in the fashion sector, which does not allow access to the general public, and where most stands belong to designers who are going to present their new collections and sell them to buyers. This means that most stands have a closed layout in order to be able to attend possible buyers in a more individualized way.

However the fair also invites design schools, art galleries, create chill-out spaces, etc.; pieces that generally have more informative and less commercial aims. This is the case for the stand of the "Escuela Superior de Moda Felicidad Duce", which exhibited work done by students.

Throughout its perimeter the stand was surrounded by hermetic stands in such a way that the passageways dissolved and different areas were created. Using this circulation space, which neighboring stands closed off, meant the designs could be arranged in groups.

The designers also resorted to formal references more commonly seen in exhibition spaces like catwalks or display windows, but without actually being either. The resulting platform had an elongated shape but was also staggered. This simultaneously brings the designs closer and further away from the spectator, combining dynamism with staticness, all aimed to exhibit each of the creations under optimal conditions; something that was overseen by fashion designer Gabriel Torres.

Design:
Narcis Font & Cristian Vivas
Photographs:
José Hevia

The designers also resorted to formal references more commonly seen in exhibition spaces like catwalks or display windows, but without actually being either. The resulting platform had an elongated shape but was also staggered.

This simultaneously brings the designs closer and further away from the spectator, combining dynamism with staticness, all aimed to exhibit each of the creations under optimal conditions; something that was overseen by fashion designer Gabriel Torres.

Park Associati

Urmet 2007

Livingluce 2007, Milan, Italy

Urmet was born in Turin, Italy, in 1937 and for decades has worked in the transformation of telecommunications, from commutation devices to intelligent terminals with evolved management concentrators. On this occasion, in keeping with the tradition and spirit that has always distinguished the group, Urmet proposes new products which feature advanced technologies, a refined and innovative aesthetic – designed by prestigious designers and architects – and simple and fast installation.

The Urmet group stand, inaugurated at Livingluce 2007 (a biennial event aimed at the home, its construction, automation, security and lighting), has been designed to present the company's image change for European trade fairs over the next three years. The project is the fruit of the collaboration between Park Associati and Studio FM, who are responsible for the company's new corporate image.

The result is a large black stage whose graphics (on the floor and the wall) guide the visitor through the products and services that the group offers. The different thematic product islands are defined by hanging cylinders of different sizes, which project a series of visually striking graphics to the exterior and, in the interior, include the display of the products. A large black parallelipid acts as a backdrop to the cylinders and accommodates the meeting rooms and the bar area.

Design:
Park Associati (Filippo Pagliani and Michele Rossi)

Photographs:
Paolo Pandullo

Associates:
Alexia Caccavella, Claudia Campana, Alice Cuteri and Sara Spimpolo

Consultants (graphic design):
Studio FM Milano

Area:
560 sqm

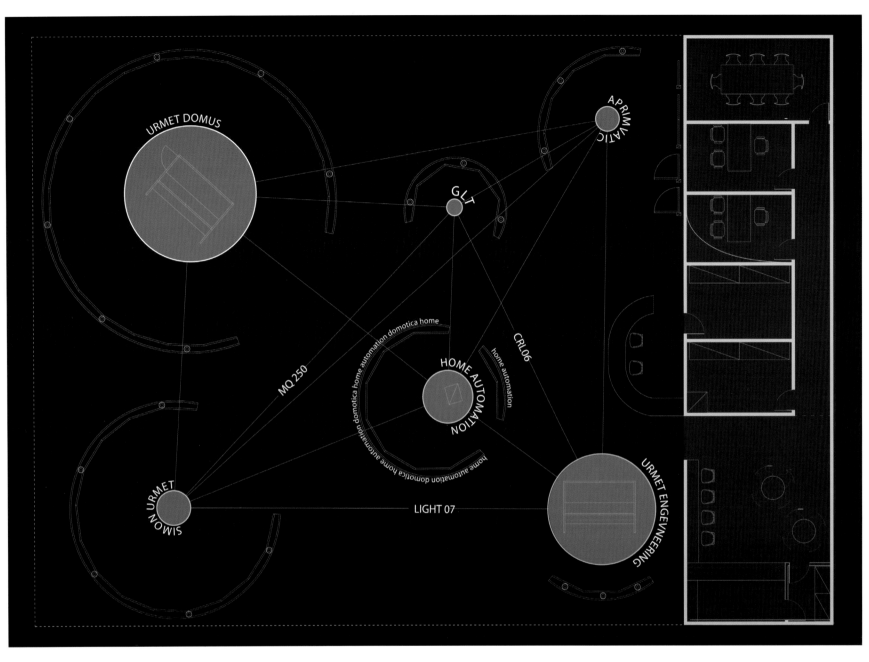

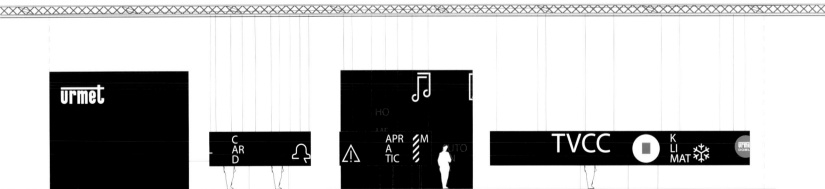

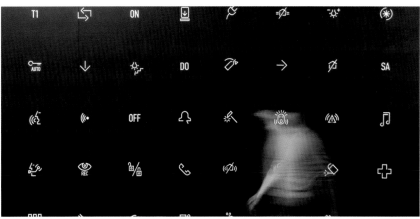

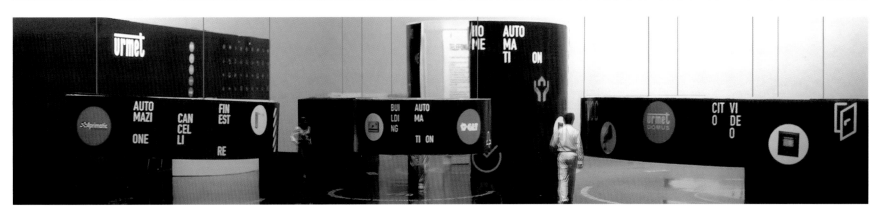

Peter Maly

Ligne Roset

IMM 2007, Cologne, Germany & Salone del Mobile 2007, Milan, Italy

A completely new exhibition architecture was conceived by designer Peter Maly for the French company Ligne Roset, one of the most highly regarded manufacturers of quality furniture. The booth was used at the international furniture show, IMM Cologne, but was designed with future exhibitions in mind as well.

A radiant transparent white exterior structure with pronounced overlapping lines comprises more than 1000 sqm (10 000 sqft) of exhibition surface area for the furniture collection. The beams join each other at different angles creating a façade that is neither closed nor open. Larger spaces indicate the most obvious places where visitors can enter the exhibition. The theme continues inside the booth through walls that divide the different areas. These have a double use as the beams can also be employed as shelving where smaller products from the company are on display. These transparent divisions allow for numerous rooms yet afford the project an increased sense of size, since visitors can always see from one end of the stand to the other. The beams that form the ceiling of the space have more regularity.

Some spaces of the booth have been set up as rooms of the house with sofas, coffee tables etc., where visitors are encouraged to 'use' the product, while others are designed simply to display the furniture. One of these areas makes use of the space above the ground. Armchairs suspended from the ceiling beams appear to float creating a magical display that serves to maximize the space as well as attracting attention and stimulating the senses.

The bar / bistro can be used as a place where visitors can relax and chat about what they have seen and also as a working space for the ligne roset team.

Design:
Peter Maly
Photographs*:
contributed by Peter Maly
*drawing below for the
Salone del Mobile, Milan, Italy
All the other photos for the
International Furniture Fair 2007, Cologne, Germany

A radiant transparent white exterior structure with pronounced overlapping lines comprises more than 1000 sqm (10 000 sqft) of exhibition surface area for the furniture collection. The beams join each other at different angles creating a façade that is neither closed nor open. Larger spaces indicate the most obvious places where visitors can enter the exhibition.

The theme continues inside the booth through walls that divide the different areas. These have a double use as the beams can also be employed as shelving where smaller products from the company are on display. These transparent divisions allow for numerous rooms yet afford the project an increased sense of size, since visitors can always see from one end of the stand to the other. The beams that form the ceiling of the space have more regularity.

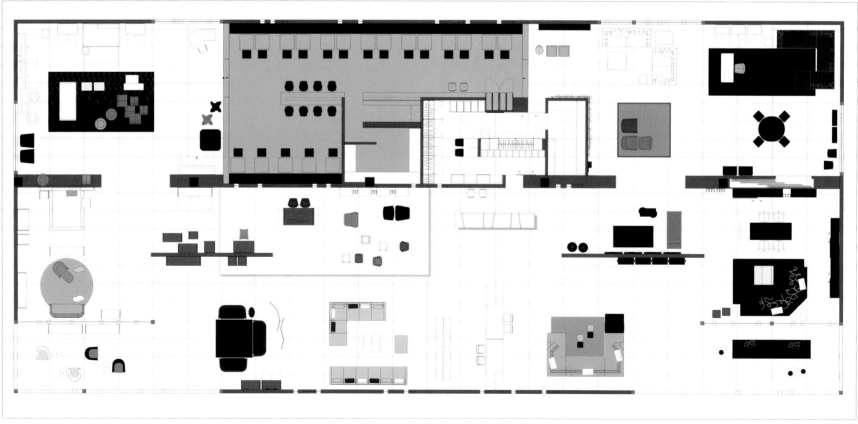

Hackenbroich Architekten

uboot.com

Online Marketing 2007, Düsseldorf, Germany

uboot.com is a company that provides an internet platform for a youth network with blogs, galleries and videos. The company sought a stand with a lounge atmosphere appropriate to the business environment, which included an innovative configuration and that would accurately represent the youth groups of social network platforms on the Internet.

The design is based on a single volume hovering above the stand. This volume consists of 1280 white textile ribbons of different lengths suspended from the ceiling. The ends of the ribbons form a surface that creates differentiated spaces with a variation of intimacies. The different 'niches' of the stand were insinuated rather than physically separated, giving visitors a sensation of coziness without feeling closed in. Beside the open space created by the ribbons, the single volume itself was permeable; the ribbons acted more like a filter than a barrier.

Tables and chairs were positioned in the center of the space while on the limits there were high tables and stools. The low chairs are made from a single piece of folded plastic, giving them the appearance that they were a part of the booth itself. A large plasma screen hanging at one end of the stand showed images related to the company's work.

The company's logo stands out sharply against the back wall, since it is the only feature in the whole stand to break with the omnipresent whiteness.

Design:
Hackenbroich Architekten
Photographs:
contributed by Hackenbroich Architekten

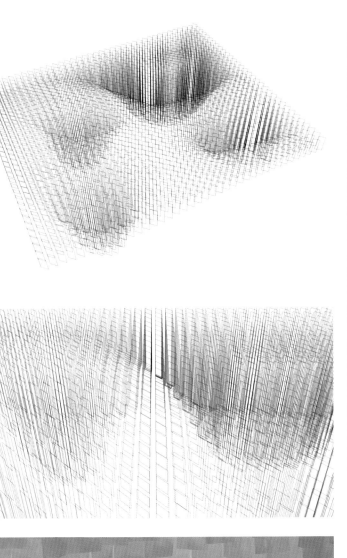

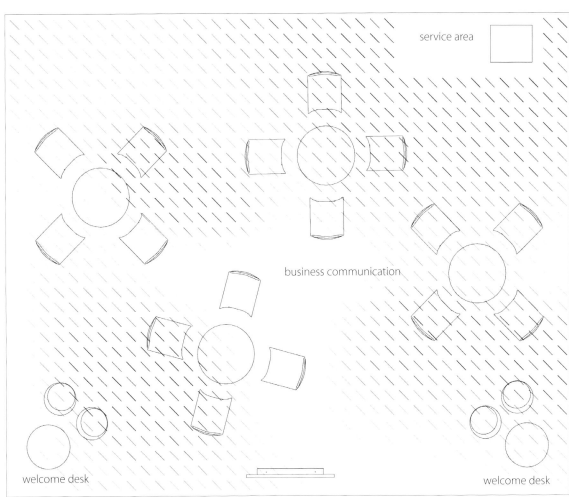

service area

business communication

welcome desk

welcome desk

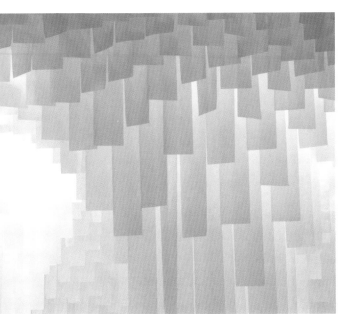

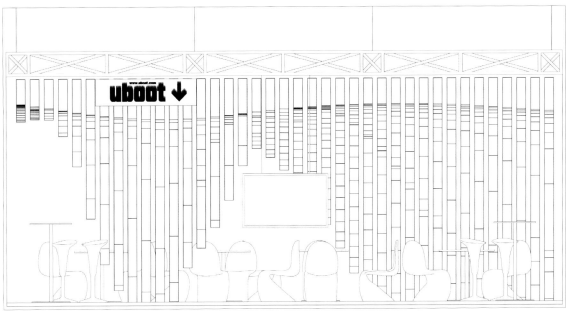

uboot ↓

D'Art Design Gruppe

Daewoo Electronics

IFA 2006, Berlin, Germany

The Berlin IFA is the world's largest Consumer Electronics trade fair and in 2006 it proved this once again by becoming the most important meeting point for the European and international sectors of electronic systems, along with a growing presence of information technology and telecommunications. With more than 1, 000 exhibitors and 225, 000 visitors, it is the world's leading sales platform of the sector.

Daewoo ranks as the world's top manufacturer of leisure and domestic electronic systems. A wide selection of visually-attractive technical products accentuates the company's trend in innovation. The basis of Daewoo Electronics' growing success is its modern, attractive designs and cutting-edge technology. The customers' interest is always of utmost importance, so Daewoo turns its imagination into advantages to this end.

The challenge facing Daewoo Electronics when planning and creating the distribution of the stand consisted of combining a wide range of products and areas of application. The objective was to present Daewoo as an innovative manufacture of electronic systems and focus on this feature in an exciting, practical showcase for the products.

The slogan of the stand was "Design meets Technology", which described not only the symbiosis between design and technology found in Daewoo's products, but also in the new organisation of the Daewoo Plaza. The designers went for clear product displays in the interior decoration, thanks to which they hit on the brand's distinguishing mark in an imaginative way.

Design:
D'Art Design Gruppe

Photographs:
contributed by D'Art Design Gruppe

Execution:
Voblo GmbH & Co. KG

Area:
1,200 sqm

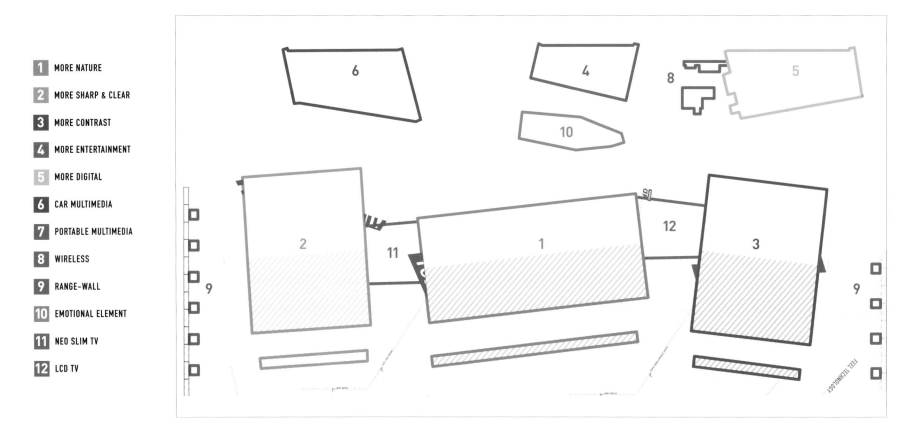

1 MORE NATURE
2 MORE SHARP & CLEAR
3 MORE CONTRAST
4 MORE ENTERTAINMENT
5 MORE DIGITAL
6 CAR MULTIMEDIA
7 PORTABLE MULTIMEDIA
8 WIRELESS
9 RANGE-WALL
10 EMOTIONAL ELEMENT
11 NEO SLIM TV
12 LCD TV

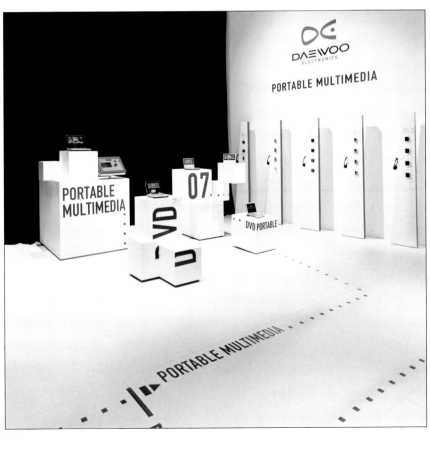

Franken Architekten

Big Bang

Mondial de l'Automobile 2006, París, France

This project shows brand architecture for the MINI World Premiere Show at the 2006 Paris Car-salon. It also shows the design of a trade fair performance and brand image that unveils a spectacular and innovative show for the world premiere of the new MINI, and at the same time confirms the existing MINI CI.

The world premiere of the new MINI will be staged as a media and spatial explosion, a 'Big Bang'. A bright red Big Bang funnel integrated into the traditional cubic black MINI brand architecture both highlights and establishes the presence of the familiar CI. This funnel stylishly puts the MINI in the limelight. The focal point of the stand is the Big Bang screen, into which the funnel-shaped space merges, and which displays various themes that focus on the brightly lit premiering vehicle.

Additional areas such as the MINI Lounge, MINI Bar, and MINI Collection Shop, as well as others, are simultaneously integrated and kept separated within the Big Bang footprint in a two-storey tract. The walls surrounding the funnel are exteriorly lit.

The lifestyle area is transformed into an Haute Couture Shop by means of luminaires and a crystal sphere that serves as a chandelier.

Design:
Franken Architekten

Photographs:
die photodesigner

Client:
BMW Group

MINI COLLECTION 2006/2007.

OPEN 24/7.
OUVERT 24 H/24
ET 7 J/7.

TIME TO GET SOME STYLE.
CHANGEZ DE STYLE.
MINI COLLECTION. AVAILABLE IN HALL 5.1.
COLLECTION MINI.

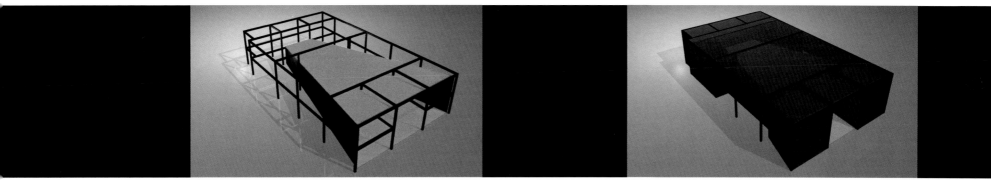

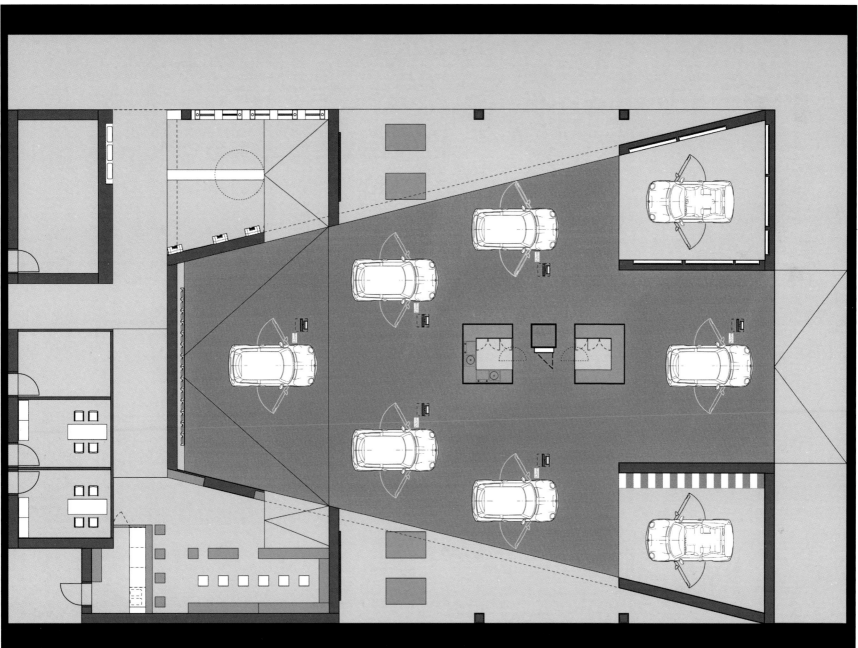

The interior design of the lounge is dominated by the momentum of the symbolic streaks of light between the seating.

For MINIPOLITANS the MINI International Wall brings major international cities to life acoustically and visually.

Josep Muñoz i Pérez

IMET

Fira Taxi 2007, Barcelona, Spain

It is the first taxi trade fair ever run and the lead time for the exhibition is short (limited to three days), so people are awaiting the results of such an event with interest.

The stand works with the logo, as it is in the subconscious of every citizen; and the colour is characteristic of Barcelona's urban landscape –a combination of black and yellow.

The emblem is transformed from two to three dimensions and scaled in order to become the support for multiple information panels. At the same time, it is designed as a singular piece in order to be reused once it is back in the office. In fact, the project of this stand introduces the concept of recycling in order to avoid that the economical investment gets reduced to just a run time of three days of exhibition. The hollowed and empty cubes can be transformed into shelves, the closed ones into office cabinets and the surfaces of all of them can be used as office boards or supports for multiple office devices such as printers, telephones, faxes, fans, etc. In addition to the main function of the exhibition modules as panel supports during the trade fair, they also take some other functions as follows: surfaces to be used as counters in order to fill the competition forms, surfaces that act as perfect seats for a short rest, shelves used as displaying racks for catalogues, modules which will function as storage cabinets, etc.

The circulations permitted within the stand are infinite, fitting all of them into different perceptions of the space. The logo repetition ensures us the retention of the exhibiting institution in the subconscious of the visitors.

Design:
Josep Muñoz i Pérez, architect

Graphic Designer:
Ferran Muñoz i Pérez

Photographs:
Sergi López Graells

Collaborators:
Élida Mosquera Marthez

Contructor:
MC Decorados, s.L.

Area:
40 sqm

The hollowed and empty cubes can be transformed into shelves, the closed ones into office cabinets and the surfaces of all of them can be used as office boards or supports for multiple office devices such as printers, telephones, faxes, fans, etc. In addition to the main function of the exhibition modules as panel supports during the trade fair, they also take some other functions as follows: surfaces to be used as counters in order to fill the competition forms, surfaces that act as perfect seats for a short rest, shelves used as displaying racks for catalogues, modules which will function as storage cabinets, etc.

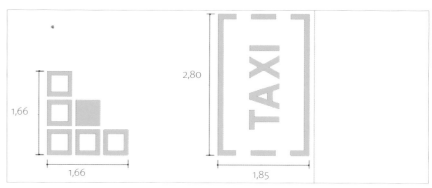

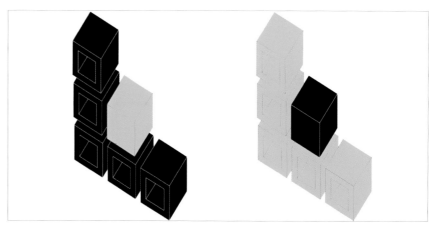

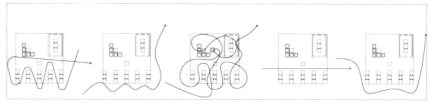

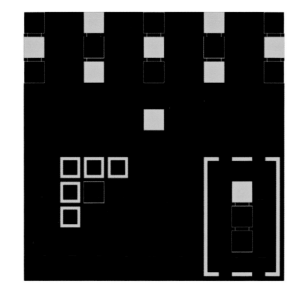

Coordination

Bogner Fire + Ice

PREMIUM, 2007, Berlin, Germany

For the presentation of the new Fire+Ice Collection at the Premium Fashion Fair in Berlin, Coordination designed an eye-catching stand that reflects Bogner's philosophy, a balance between sports and luxury.

45 square meters (480 sqft) of bright, white reflective surfaces, as radiant as the snow on a clear winter day, remind the visitor of a ski slope. Two red dynamic stripes on the otherwise white PVC floor and on the high-gloss white back wall evoke the speed of downhill skiing, while a huge clear-blue 4-cubic meter (140 cubic foot) ice display allows visitors to actually feel the winter cold as well as being symbolic of the second half of the brand's name. The ice block, in combination with a slope made from the same material as the floor, conjures up the image of a ramp such as those used by snowboarders for performing jumps and tricks.

This display, consisting of crushed ice in between two ice block walls with the brand name apparently embedded inside, is connected to the communication counter made of white powder coated aluminum, where two monitors embedded in a chrome frame provide a possibility for interaction and also show Fire+Ice promotional films.

The stand has plenty of space, in particularly in relation to the amount of product on display, so visitors can wander around freely without bumping into each other. A small detail, a carefully placed piece of fur on the showcase gives this cool and sporty trade fair stand just the right touch of warmth.

Design:
Coordination Ausstellungs GmbH
Photographs:
diephotodesigner.de
Area:
45 sqm (480 sqft)

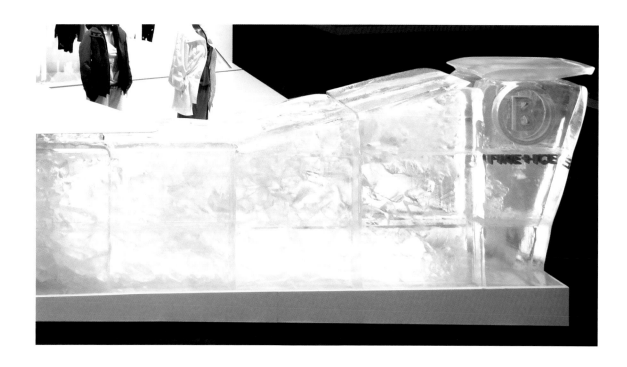

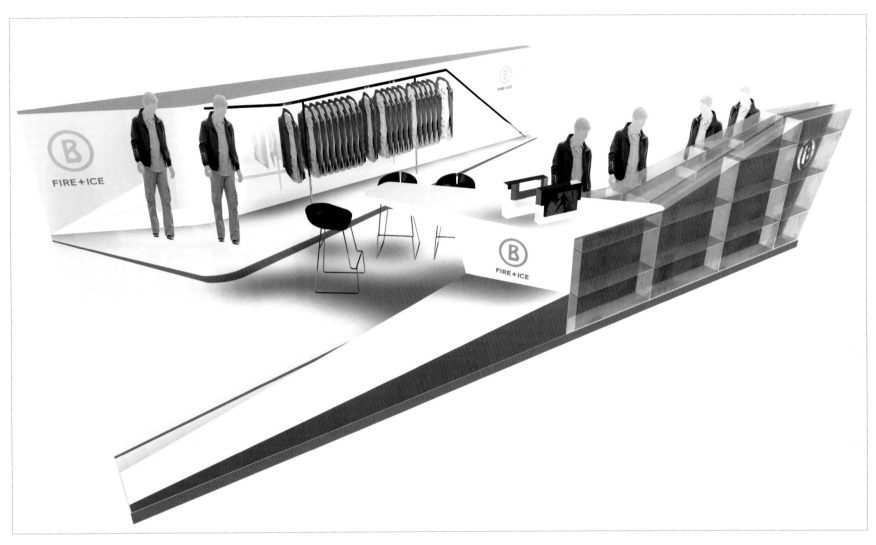

The stand has plenty of space, in particularly in relation to the amount of product on display, so visitors can wander around freely without bumping into each other. A small detail, a carefully placed piece of fur on the showcase gives this cool and sporty trade fair stand just the right touch of warmth.

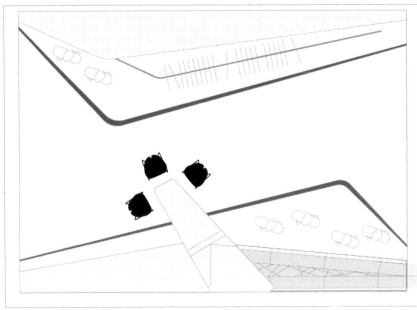

Cricursa

Construmat 2007, Barcelona, Spain

The architects started out with silica, raw material for the creation of glass, which appears in numerous minerals such as quartz, in crystalline formations that generate polyhedral volumes threaded within one another, stemming from the same base and generating spaces between its parts. These structures are the personification of the type of architecture this group strives for; an architectural scene of union between man and nature.

From the application of the program to this digital geode, as it goes from the boardroom to the product area, the audiovisual area, and to the warehouse, a cut and moulded geometry comes forth following an analogous process similar to that which a jeweller would use in the shaping of a diamond, giving worth and order to each of the distinct parts that comprise the project. The definition of the constructive process represents the step from virtual to real. Each of the materials has its concrete characteristics: weight, resistance, maximum production dimensions, etc. The definitive model comes from these premises as much in form as its constructive system. It deals with a structure based upon a stainless steel plate frame folded and screwed on in order to make a stable mesh capable of supporting the weight of the glass panes. The panes, placed like clasping elements on the mesh, bond the structure. This way they go from simple ornamentation to structural function.

Design:
Jordi Fernández & Eduardo Gutiérrez / ON-A

Photographs:
Lluis Ros

Collaborators:
Jordi Farell, Carlos García-Sancho / ON-A

Graphic design:
Bernardo Magalhaes / ON-A

Structure engineer:
CRICURSA technical department

Multimedia application:
GROTESK

Glass and metal structure:
CRICURSA

Acid etching and vinyls :
GRABACID

Carpentry:
CALPEMA

Carpeting:
SERINKJET

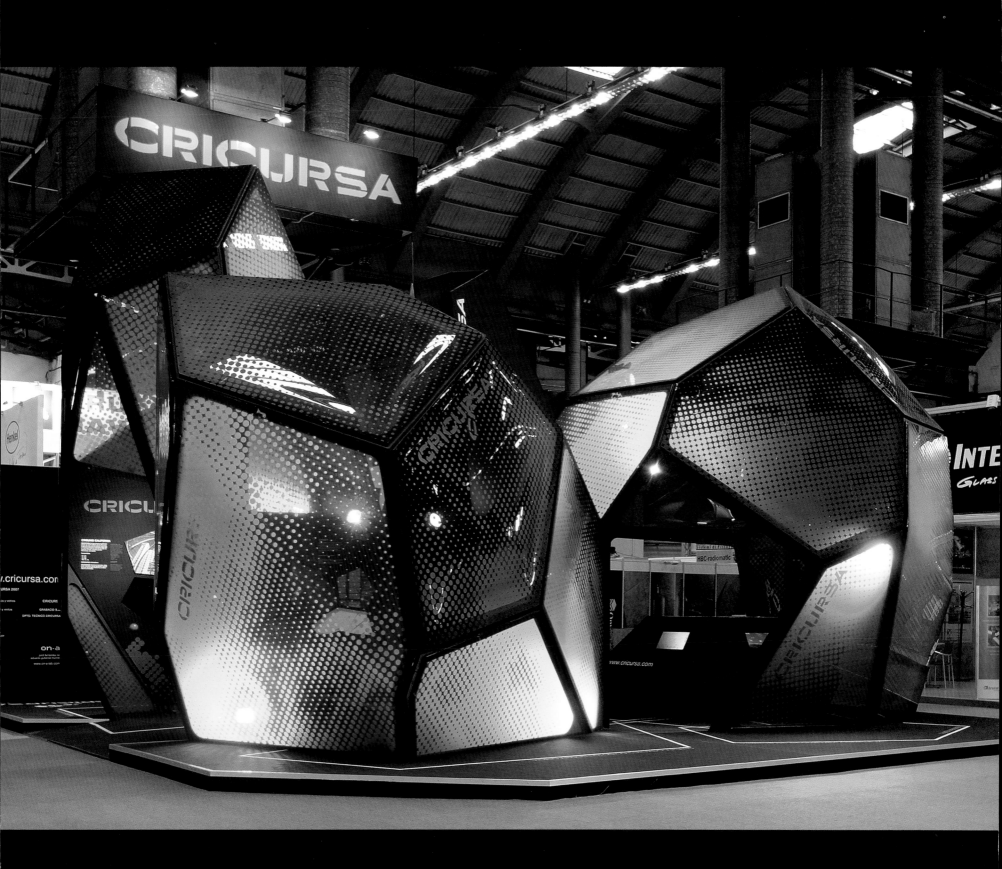

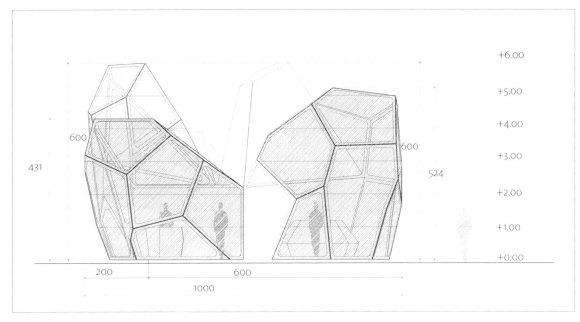

Three different types of glass are differentiated in the project according to their corporative colours. On one side we have the yellow-orange flat panes and the orange folded ones that make two distinct planes, united through a curve. On the other side we have the blue spheres with a convex surface in which the central arrow reaches up to twenty centimetres. All of the glass panes have different forms and are acid engraved with a pattern achieving a greater variety of transparencies from one end to the next.

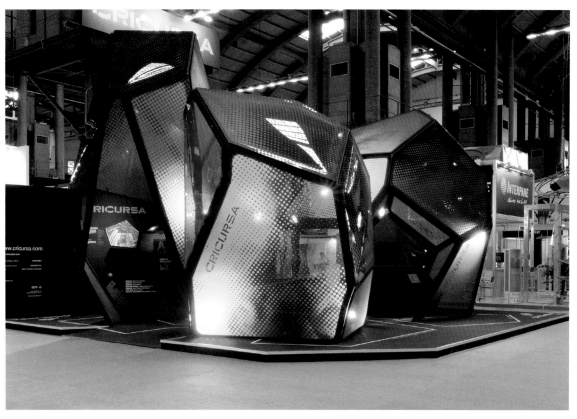

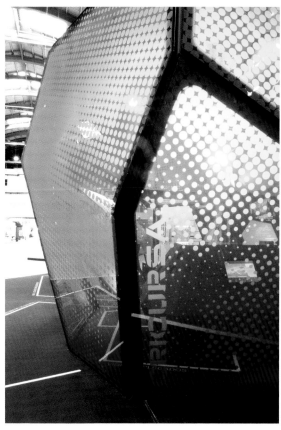

Winntech

Winntech

Global Shop 2007, Las Vegas, USA

The design strategy adopted by the Winntech team for the 2007 edition of GlobalShop was: "Stop Gawk and Ask". Faced with the task of creating a presence that would elicit this visceral response from convention visitors, the creative team came up with the idea of using super graphics to announce their presence at GlobalShop 2007.

From the moment you entered the Convention Center, you couldn't help but be drawn to The Pig. And The Wolf. Back-to-back imagery proclaiming Winntech's design approach to serving their clients. Winntech used a huge 15 m (50 ft) wide, two-sided banner that stretched 9 m (30 ft) high as the back of its booth. One side featured a pig's head with red lips and beady eyes along with the text, "@!#% Ordinary," while the other side displayed a wolf and the words "Abandon Fear." Take chances. Avoid the usual. Seek your own voice. A highly effective way to simultaneously get noticed and transmit a message. In addition to the graphics Winntech intentionally kept the booth brand free, in order to generate curiosity.

Along with the two 140 sqm (1500 sqft) graphics, Winntech designed and built 4 client meeting stations complete with 130 cm (50 in) flat panel touch screens, red leather club seating, and dry ice beverage coolers.

The result of this design strategy was that more registered visitors than any other single show in Winntech history came to the stand. Furthermore this hard-hitting imagery appealed to a wider audience than previous years.

Design:
Winntech

Photographs:
contributed by Winntech

"STOP GAWK AND ASK"

o!#%   ORDINARY

HELP IS ON THE WAY™

representative sketch

The result of this design strategy was that more registered visitors than any other single show in Winntech history came to the stand. Furthermore this hard-hitting imagery appealed to a wider audience than previous years.

Schmidhuber + Partner

Audi

Design Annual 2006, Frankfurt, Germany

For the most design-oriented of the German premium auto brands, it was a true premiere: for the first time, Audi participated in the „The Design Annual" in Frankfurt. Adapting to the exhibition motto „inside:urban", the Audi TT was staged as a modern nomad, created for the urban environment and at home all over the world. It doesn't need a garage, but a house made specifically for it. We conceived the booth as a largely closed body, with a monolithic character that can be experienced through its wall thickness and its matte, dark, hard materiality. In the interior, fully covered with soft, white rubber material, color and feel are reversed. Urbanistas were able to relax, talk and enjoy the „Making of Audi TT" film with their headphones in the media niche. A window was projected on the media horizon that symbolized the view from the TT house and conveyed urbanity à la Audi TT to the visitors. Eleven international photo artists designed the views, while the Berlin videojockeys, BAUHOUSE, rolled out the appropriate image and sound carpet.

Design:
Concept and architecture by
Schmidhuber + Partner, Munich

Photographs:
Christoph Vohler, Munich

Client:
AUDI AG, Ingolstadt

Communication:
Mutabor Design GmbH, Hamburg

Lighting:
Four to One: scale design, Hürth

Assembly:
Ambrosius Messebau GmbH,
Frankfurt a. Main

Constructed surface area:
125 sqm

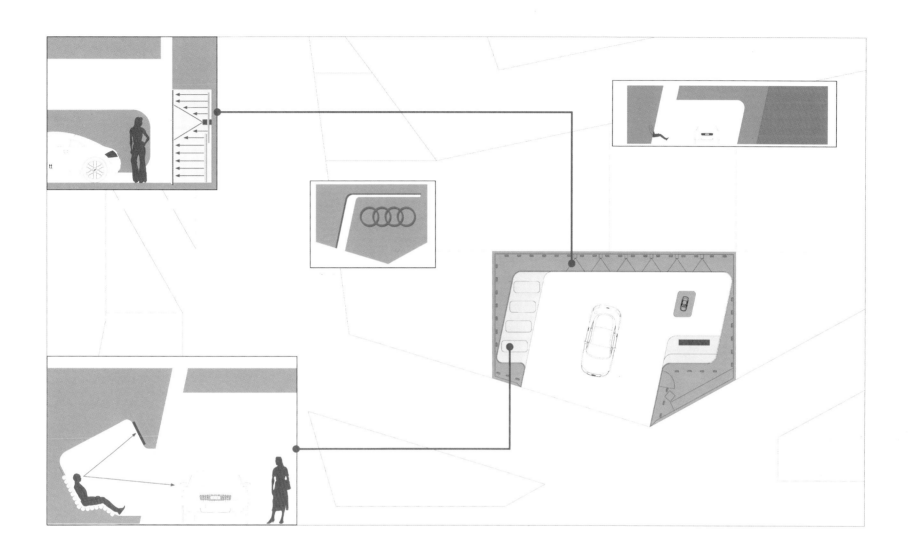

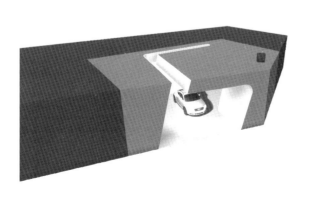

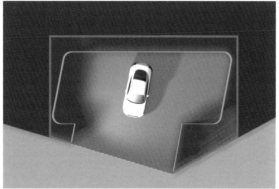

The architecture is derived from the typical anatomy of the Audi TT; a new mix of radial forms with sharp angles that discovers the union of curves and corners.

The stand has been created as a closed but spacious assembly of areas (display area, video area and lounge) that presents its solidity in the visible thickness of its walls and durability of its materials. Its monolithic character is reinforced with a dark, matte exterior wall made of hard materials.

ecru ag

ZMV

Berufsmesse 2007, Zurich, Switzerland

The master painters and plasterers guild of Zurich (ZMV) has fostered improvements on the professional artisans' stand. The slogan "the creative ones in construction" has reinforced its professional image. The ZMV has promoted measures that point the professional toward new aspirations. The new stand focused its aim on expressing the current change from craftsman to creative worker.

It is becoming increasingly difficult for craftsmen to find and educate qualified personnel. This is because of the antiquated image that persists in this type of profession. The new stand should actively transmit the qualified work of the artisans, and above all be directed at possible apprentices. It approached them with demonstrations of the craft and valuable examples— showing the profession from all sides.

The objective was to create a new guide for this professional field with this stand. Its organization spanned all the regional activity of the guild. It must function as an orientative stand for many years, with a lasting effect.

It fulfilled many diverse functions. First of all, it encouraged the visitor to actively participate in the activity being carried out by the artisans. Booths were created for this activity in which they displayed finished, high quality aesthetic craftwork pieces. On the other side, one could actively follow a craftsman in the construction process. Behind it, in the background, a room was created to share information and carry out specialized consultations, as well as offer the possibility to participate in a contest.

The stand attracted 43,000 visitors in five days. The perception of master painters and plasterers changed as much for the visitors as well as the guild itself, forever.

Design:
ecru ag Zürich, Thomas Wachter

Photography:
Brigitte Richi

Collaborator:
Sascha Däschler

Area:
100 sqm

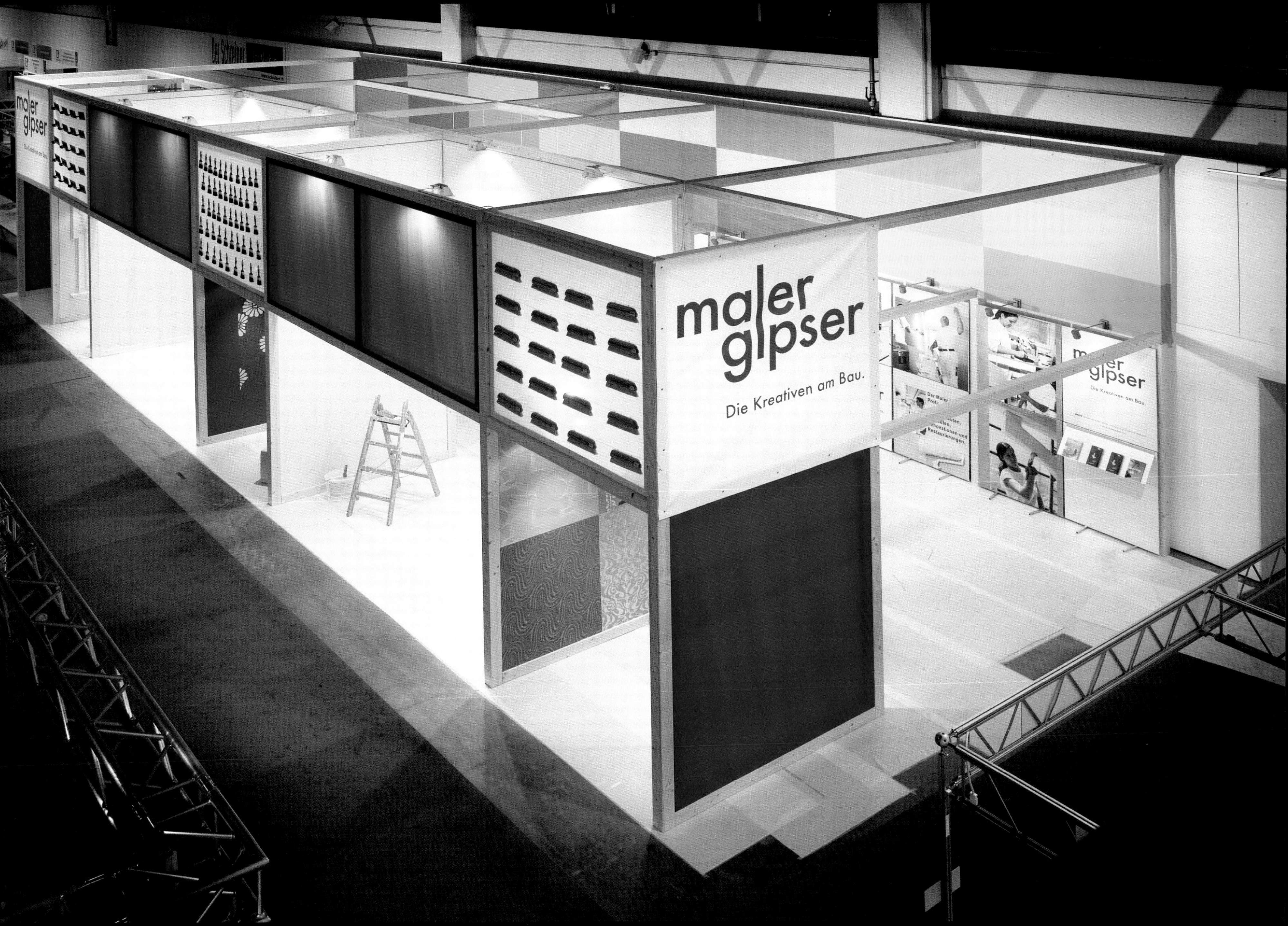
maler
gipser
Die Kreativen am Bau.

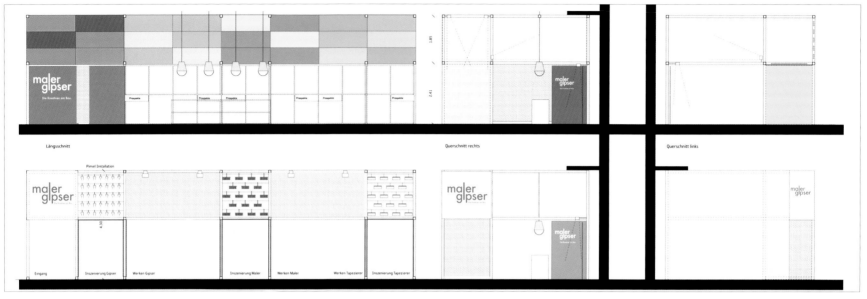

Längsschnitt Querschnitt rechts Querschnitt links

166

ARNO Design

Sto AG

Farbe - Ausbau & Fassade 2007, Cologne, Germany

Sto is renowned as the market leading supplier of high quality renders and external wall insulation systems to the construction industry. The company also specializes in products that cover a wide range of construction needs, such as façade and interior paints. Sto AG was awarded the "Top 100" seal of quality for outstanding innovation management in the area of façade design, as one of the 100 most innovative German enterprises in 2006 and 2007. This was the motivation behind Arno Design's intention to try new tracks in the façade design for the exhibition stand at the "Farbe - Ausbau & Fassade 2007" exhibition.

The booth was completely designed in the colors that make up the brand image; white and yellow. Transparent thread curtains gave the space a compact appearance, as well as one of exclusiveness and intimacy, while at the same time allowing visitors to easily enter to see and explore what was inside.

Information and catering areas were laid out as independent modules, the floor area of which exactly corresponded to the yellow bar of the Sto logo. This succinct element also provided color and form for the side walls and presentation elements of the stand.

Podiums were equipped with laptops where visitors could sit on stools and find out more about the company products. All around the stand screens also showed images depicting the company's product range and philosophy. Poufs, again in the company's trademark yellow, were scattered about the space, allowing people to rest their legs and remain within the boundaries of the stand and within sight of the informative screens.

Design:
ARNO Design
Photographs:
Frank Kotzerke/ ARNO ©
Area:
695 sqm

170

Podiums were equipped with laptops where visitors could sit on stools and find out more about the company products. All around the stand screens also showed images depicting the company's product range and philosophy. Poufs, again in the company's trademark yellow, were scattered about the space, allowing people to rest their legs and remain within the boundaries of the stand and within sight of the informative screens.

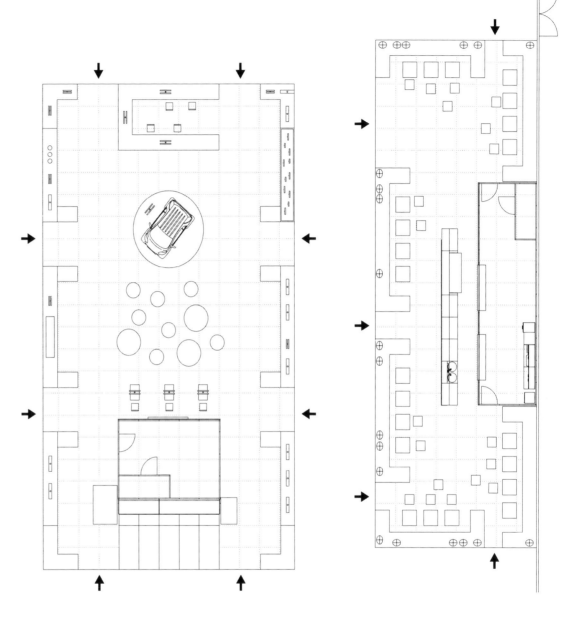

Schmidhuber + Partner

Grohe AG

ISH 2007, Frankfurt, Germany

The brand Grohe Water Technology emerges renovated at the ISH 2007 and unveils its new slogan "Enjoy Water!" that displays a change in its brand strategy.

Continuing the efficient use of the jets as a presentation element for the 2005 product, they will use the concept and content on the 2007 fair entrance as well. The protagonists of the ceiling design that introduce the new blue CI are the "streams" formed by hanging and oscillating strings that recreate the water's movement.

In the stand, visitors are welcomed with drinks and hors d'oeuvres in an open welcome lounge and bar, which strikes a clear contrast with the product presentation area through the use of green colour tones.

The fundamental idea of the GROHE fairs—beyond the ISH 2007—stems from a modular organization so that the corporate design can be applied to all other GROHE fair formats; from presentation of the most important products to the most functional faucets.

In summary, the unmistakable image of the 2005-2007 GROHE stands can be proven to be most adequate and have successfully strengthened the brand. The emotional charge of the 2007 stand comes from contact with the client through the presentation of the most outstanding products and the creation of the welcome lounge. This way, the sum of all parts achieves an effective presentation of GROHE's new slogan: Enjoy Water!

Design:
Schmidhuber + Partner, Munich

Photographs:
Wolfgang Oberle, Munich

Client:
Grohe AG, Hemer

Lighting:
Four to one: scale design, Hürth

Lighting technology:
LK Lichtdesign & Klangkonzept, Essen

Assembly:
Werbe- und Messebau Walbert-Schmitz, Aachen

Overhead fixtures and structure:
Procedes, Lemwerder
(jets and whirlpools)

Area:
38 x 31m / 1.178 sqm

GROHE Showers
every drop is full of enjoyment

In this occasion a suitable environment is created for the presentation of the best products by placing the whirlpools at the central axis, which focuses the view on outstanding elements through means of form, lighting and colour. Water is used below the "whirlpools" to create the shower and kitchen environments.

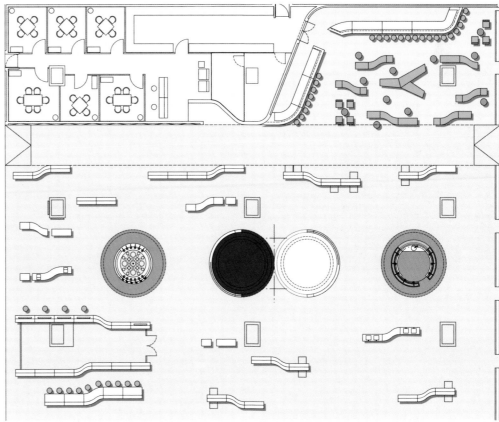

The new Ondus faucet series occupies a highlighted position in the presentation with its contrasts between black and white and its new forms, representing a turning point in the development of Grohe products.

GROHE Ondus

GROHE Ondus sprengt Grenzen, indem sie mutig minimalistische Einfachheit und Emotionen verbindet. Das Ergebnis ist eine Kollektion mit Kultstatus. Entdecken Sie bei GROHE den "sinnlichen Minimalismus". Lassen Sie sich von einer völlig neuen Formensprache faszinieren.

GROHE Ondus stands alone as a bold aesthetic statement, daring to evolve the geometric boundaries of form. This iconic new collection was created following the 'Sensual Minimalism' philosophy, which defines the beauty of simplicity with emotion.

Totems + urbanberry design

Julius Zöllner

Kind und Jugent 2004, Cologne, Germany

The trade fair in Cologne in 2004, "Kind und Jugent" is one of the biggest events for Julius Zöllner, a company that produces baby products such as bottles, quilts, beds, toys, etc. Consequently they commissioned the Holland and Japan based design team Urbanberry to come up with a platform that would stand out at the event and convey the company's corporate philosophy. The stand concept is "bloom", an action associated with the notion of "growing tenderly", which can be applied both to the company's customers and to the company itself. The stand occupies a surface area of around 29 x 12.5 m (95 x 41 ft).

A paper curtain has been positioned gently in the center of the space, which acts as a partition. This division is semi-transparent since it is composed of strips of paper that have been assembled to form diamond shaped hollows. It moves softly when people pass by and the thin slices of paper rub against each other creating the almost imperceptible sound of paper-to-paper friction. This audio effect, according to the designers of the stand, is reminiscent of a light breeze blowing through a field of grass. It transmits a feeling of fragility, associated with the company's target customers.

Tables used throughout the stand as a display system, a place from which to serve the complementary beverages and as a decorative element, create a homely environment for visitors. Spotlights positioned above these spaces create circles of light around the tables, which in turn create shadow patterns on the floor that resemble flower petals.

Design:
Totems + urbanberry

Photographs:
contributed bt urbanberry

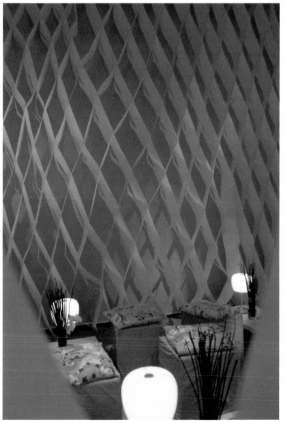

bachmann.kern & partner

Tatung

IFA 2007, Berlin, Germany

Design:
bachmann.kern & partner

Photographs:
contributed by bachmann.kern & partner

Tatung Netherlands b.v. is the European branch of the Tatung headquarters based in Taiwan.

The company is a worldwide leader in the design and production of a vast array of digital consumer products, including LCD-TVs and PDPs, network-connected devices, etc.

The challenge for IFA 2007 in Berlin, the world's largest consumer electronics trade fair, was to enhance the publicity of the Tatung brand in Europe, to get in touch with new clients and to develop their customer relations.

The subject matter for this booth was "100-hertz and 90 years of Tatung". At the request of Tatung, complicated multimedia-presentations and complex engineering were not included in the stand design. Communicating the 100-hertz-technology without any complex engineering was the most difficult challenge. 100-hertz-technology projects an image onto a TV-screen at twice the speed as its predecessor, 50-hertz. Half pictures are projected a hundred times a second with the result that you don't get any flickering pictures. Even with a big screen each picture is defined and clear. The innovative design concept applied here symbolizes this technology, and although on arrival visitors may not have seen how the stand 'worked', a closer examination soon revealed all.

The Tatung history-timeline was applied to the floor in the red that characterized the entire stand. A red circle was painted on a point along this line, which represented 46 years of Tatung – when the company exported its first TVs to Europe. A series of walls were placed one behind the other shaped in a very specific way so that when visitors stood on this red circle the 100-hertz in front of them became clear and defined. This interactive element generated a positive and exciting experience for visitors as well as being informative and fun. Aside from this main feature, the stand was of simple design, the red on the white background creating a clearly defined contrast. A group of plasma screens at the front of the stand were arranged next to some red stools, where visitors could sit and watch the images.

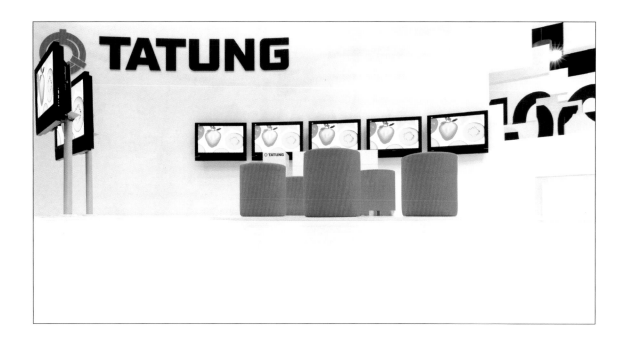

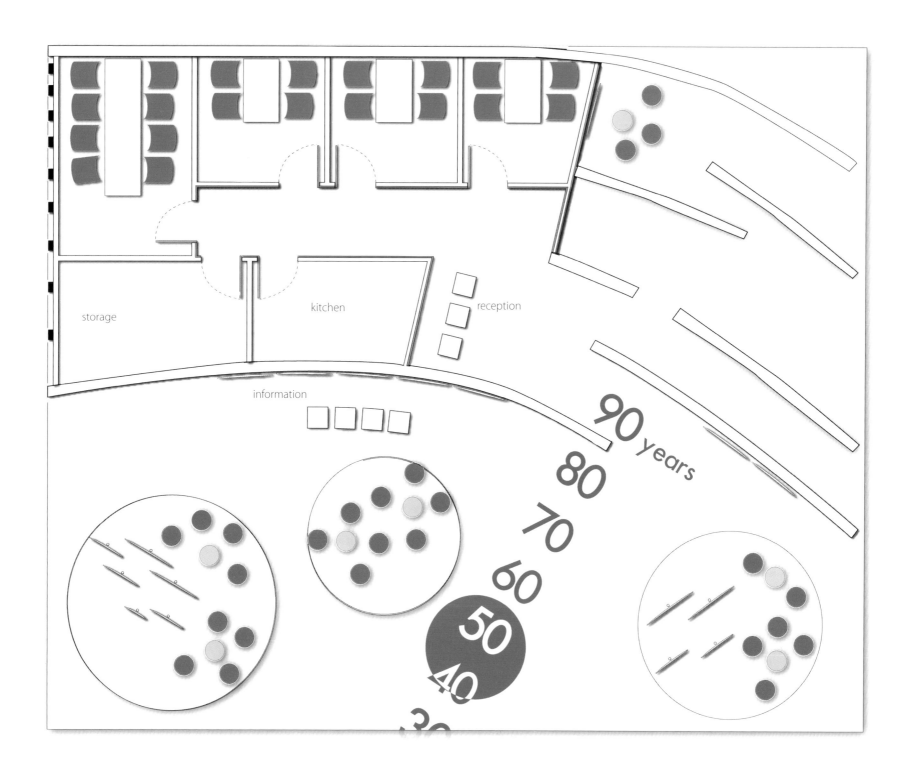

storage

kitchen

reception

information

90 years
80
70
60
50
40
30

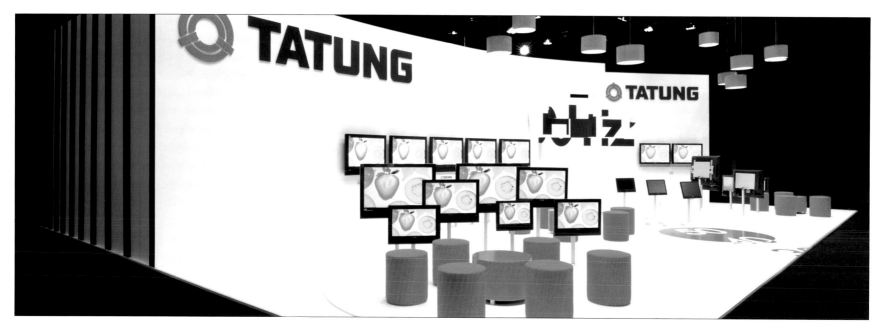

Manuel Torres Acemel

Grupo Gres Catalán

Construmat 2007, Barcelona, Spain

Grupo Gres Catalán commissioned designer Manuel Torres with the global creation of their self-supporting stand at Barcelona's International Building Exhibition, the 'Construcción Construmat'.

The plan consisted in the elaboration of an integral design for the space in question, starting with the structure, the layout, the selection of materials that the company offers, the lighting, the graphics, the finishing materials, the industrial design of elements for specific uses and needs, as well as the arrangement of materials and props that had to be on display, thus exhibiting the event's content and of course its leitmotif. Lastly and most importantly the global configuration of the design had to be able to represent Grupo Gres Catalán in seven international trade fairs of different surface areas and with different positions within the fair, whilst maintaining the same aesthetical concept, multi-usefulness and effective use of the elements projected. The stand is presented as a solid parallelepiped with proportional volumes and has an intimate and elegant appearance. Its layout develops practically and fluidly through a symmetric articulation, where the visitor is received in the main entrance module, and makes his way through to the different exhibition modules. The chromatics offer the stand a contemporary, elegant and neutral atmosphere, alternating chiaroscuro with reflections provided by the different materials. The items on display were thus allowed to be the focal point of the stand.

The lighting, via spotlights and indirect lighting, was a vital component in order to enhance the final products and avoid distorting their differences, tones and textures.

This is a contemporary, symmetric and lightweight design, able to harmonize the technical requirements with aesthetics and including different types of details in order to achieve a practical modular system and an atmosphere full of sensations.

Design:
Manuel Torres Acemel

Photographs:
Ginger Studio BCN, Mar Mateu & Victor Celdrán

Area:
340 sqm

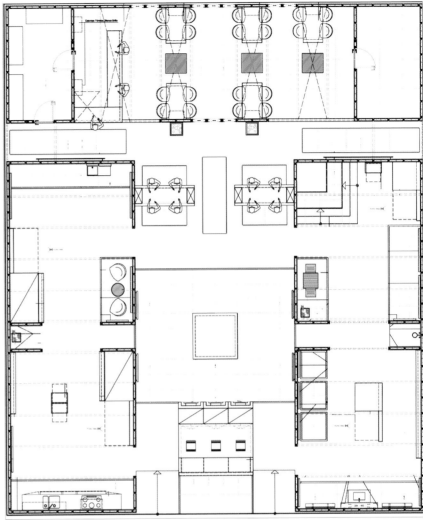

Quinze & Milan

Quinze & Milan

Salone del Mobile 2007, Milan, Italy

The Salone del Mobile Internazionale is the International Furniture Fair of Milan, the largest and most anticipated trade fair of its kind. It is renowned as the leading exposition for new products by furniture manufacturers and designers. Quinze & Milan's stand at the event's 2007 edition stood out for its playful, urban atmosphere.

The virtue of the design of this stand is its simplicity. It allows the products on display to do all the talking, since it is virtually free of any objects that could obstruct the views.

Arne Quinze hand-painted the graphics on the white walls and floor himself. These recreate the items of furniture on display in two dimensions. In turn the furniture has been placed apparently at random around the booth. One of the overriding images is the honeycomb-flexible shelving system, a structure designed by Clive Wilkinson that can grow as more pieces are added. The designer's head also features on the wall, welcoming people to the lounge area. The drawings are more like rough sketches and include small sections of text, written by the designer. The style is reminiscent of the design process itself, reminder visitors of the uniqueness of the products as well as the work that has to be done before they are produced. Shelves seemingly floating on the walls support chairs and stools of different designs.

Steps lead up to a platform at one end where chairs and tables offer an informal lounge area, where visitors can rest, exchange ideas and find out more information regarding the items on display.

Design & concept:
Arne Quinze

Photographs:
Thierry van Dort for Quinze & Milan

Construction:
Quinze & Milan

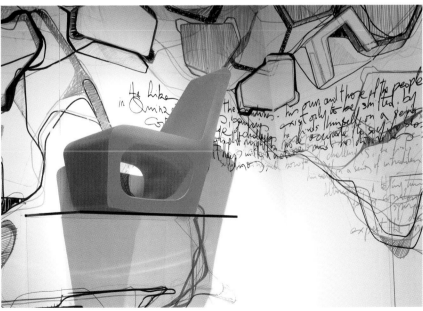

Carlos Martínez

Egokiefer

SWISSBAU 2005, Basel, Switzerland

One of EgoKiefer's main aims regarding their presentation at the trade fair was to reach the different target groups in all regions of Switzerland and make both the company and the brand name "EgoKiefer" better known through their new stand concept. The company's philosophy is "improving quality of life", and thanks to this they have reached the top of the Swiss window market. Their objective in this fair was simply to make this position known.

The important thing was that visitors take something away from the stand. They had to have an effective experience in different ways: the atmosphere, the interaction, the surprises and impressions with the help of light, color, music and video all helped to achieve this goal. Furthermore a reproduction of the company history and information about the products encouraged people to stay.

The architectural theme chosen for the stand is fluctuating space, which is produced in both the horizontal and vertical areas. Moving from the lower floor to the upper one is resolved by way of a ramp that is part of the complete visit to the stand by the public. All guests are treated like kings here; the reduction in hierarchies regarding the different types of visitors is an important psychological aspect of the project.

The stand is accessed by a step, which takes visitors to a large platform, the display stage and a room without walls. The ramp constitutes the gradual change to the upper floor, which opens slowly to the changing perspectives of the stand as well as the rest of the fair.

Design:
Carlos Martinez

Photographs:
Peter Hauck

Area:
ground floor, 315 sqm
1th floor, 128 sqm

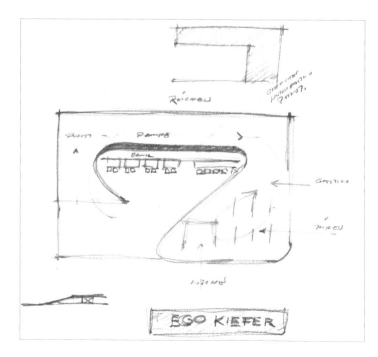

The architectural theme chosen for the stand is fluctuating space, which is produced in both the horizontal and vertical areas. Moving from the lower floor to the upper one is resolved by way of a ramp that is part of the complete visit to the stand by the public. All guests are treated like kings here; the reduction in hierarchies regarding the different types of visitors is an important psychological aspect of the project.

Berlin meets Tokyo

Spiral Garden Omotesando, 2006, Tokyo, Japan

This stand was presented at the Special Exhibition of Berlin Fashion Design at the Spiral Garden Omotesando in Tokyo.
With its unique mix of different atmospheres, neighborhoods and cultures, the city of Berlin has a great appeal to creative people from all over the world. Berlin has a lively Design and Fashion Scene with reciprocal influence and exchange between designers from all disciplines; over time, a multi-faceted "Berlin Style" has emerged. The booth has been designed to reflect this tendency.

The exhibition at the Spiral Garden in Tokyo presents outfits of the current in-style Berlin Fashion Labels Sisi Wasabi, Lala Berlin, 30 paar-haende, von Wedel & Tiedeken, Macqua, Presque Fini and c.neeon.

For this occasion, the exhibition designers of Coordination Berlin have created a Fashion / Design Environment in which the special "Berlin Feeling" can be experienced. A 250 sqm (2700 sqft) graphic carpet unfolds across the floor and up the walls. Above, the outfits, just flown in from the runways of Milan and Paris, hover on 13m (42 ft) long ropes. The large printed carpet shows typical scenes of Berlin city life: Next to the television tower on Alexanderplatz one finds the Berlin bear, a Döner Kebab vendor and much more. The artwork for this was created by the young Berlin Graphic Design team "Jacques et Brigitte".

On one of the 3 "Dialounge" – loungers, visitors can browse through Berlin Fashion and Lifestyle Magazines. Coordination has transformed the Spiral Garden into a melting pot, in which Graphics, Fashion and space melt into unity. Visitors are invited to go on a discovery quest which has been designed to offer a strong impression of what the trend workshop in Berlin has to offer. The overall appearance of the stand conveys a feeling of eclecticism that reflects the current fashion scene in the German capital.

Design:
Coordination Ausstellungs GmbH

Photographs:
Tomo Yamaguchi

Artwork:
Jacqueset Brigitte

Client / Initiators:
Goethe Institut Tokyo
Premium Exhibitions GmbH
Berlinomat
Pabst Fashion Concepts
Create Berlin e.V.

Supporters:
Partner für Berlin

Area:
300 sqm

Artek

Ford

Autoshow 2007, Buenos Aires, Argentina

In the style of futurism and based on the work of Giacomo Balla (more precisely on his work, "volo di rondini"), the pavilion stands as a tribute to the movement.

A visually interrupted superposition of layers ensures the dynamics of the space, using the spectator as a mobile generator to all the action.

The existence of two faces, a physical one (at the front) and a graphical one (at the back) with different resolutions directs the gaze towards a surface that does not exist, that evolves and is formed as a result of both faces and is forever moving. A permanent stroboscope, which depends on the movement of the on-looker.

In this ocean of endless connections, today's vehicles (like the machines of futurism in the 1900s) are displayed in all their visual prowess, a fitting frame for the machine of the future.

Design:
Artek

Stand surface area

Photographs:
contributed by Artek

Area:
2000 sqm

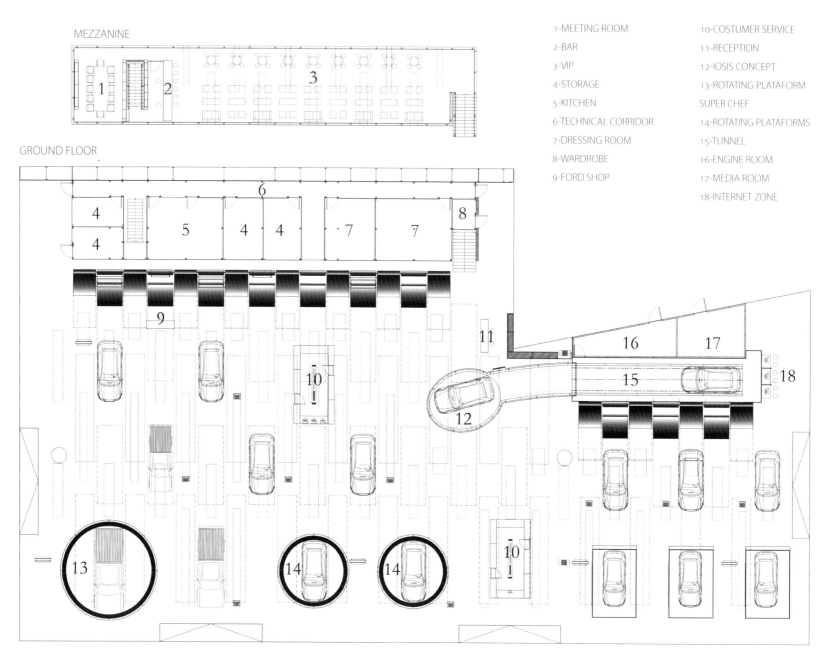

MEZZANINE

GROUND FLOOR

1-MEETING ROOM
2-BAR
3-VIP
4-STORAGE
5-KITCHEN
6-TECHNICAL CORRIDOR
7-DRESSING ROOM
8-WARDROBE
9-FORD SHOP

10-COSTUMER SERVICE
11-RECEPTION
12-IOSIS CONCEPT
13-ROTATING PLATAFORM
SUPER CHEF
14-ROTATING PLATAFORMS
15-TUNNEL
16-ENGINE ROOM
17-MEDIA ROOM
18-INTERNET ZONE

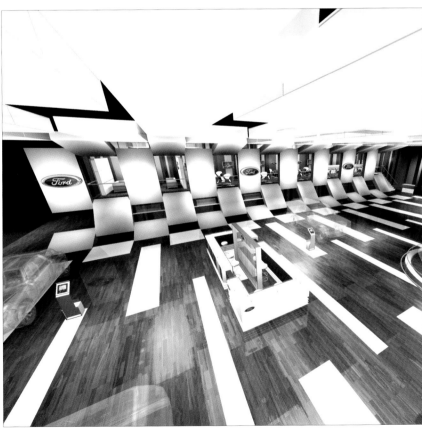

Migliore+Servetto Architetti Associati

BTicino

Livinluce 2007, Milan, Italy

BTicino brings the value of quality, technology and, above all, Italian design to more than 60 countries and it does so by introducing the recognised values of aesthetics and comfort to the field of functional features and installations. These factors have guided the firm towards a new design concept through the study of forms, materials and colours. But design for BTicino is not only an instrument of decoration, but a way to participate in a project with innovative solutions, and influence the user's quality of work and life. Since 1989, BTicino has formed part of the multinational company Legrand, a worldwide leader in electric equipment for low tension installations. The firm's concept is transmitted to Livinluce's visitors through an ensemble project which, in a large space (3,500m2 or 37,634.41sqft), shows us the firms and products of Bticino, Legrand, Zucchini and Otronics through the definition of a unified image, although deeply versatile.

The closed perimeter of the space is opened in a wide reception entrance that guides the flow of visitors towards an interior circular plaza 15 meters (50ft) in diameter. At the same time, the plaza acts as a presentation space for Gruppo with central dynamic 360° projections. It also acts as a radial centre of orientation through which pathways and exposition sites are defined with wide and surprising perspectives.The urban installations are stark and simple, comprising a source of light and graphic as well as chromatic communication. They are structured as to the long views proportioned in perspective to the 7-metre-tall pillars, visible even from outside the closed boundaries of the stand.

Beyond the central plaza we find the bar area which consists of a second meeting point between the diverse exposition areas. It is a walkway, meeting and pause place with a privileged overlooking view of the entire complex from a height of approximately a metre and a half (5ft).

Three installations with other products from the multinational company Legrand characterise the space dedicated to this firm.

Design:
Migliore+Servetto Architetti Associati
Ico Migliore, Mara Servetto

Photographs:
Paolo Pandullo

Collaborators:
Tania Giorgi, Matteo Mocchi,
Cristina Tomada, Yu-Fung Ling,
Laurent Léon, Francesca de Giorgi

Graphic:
Studio FM Milano

Builder:
Eurofiere Spa

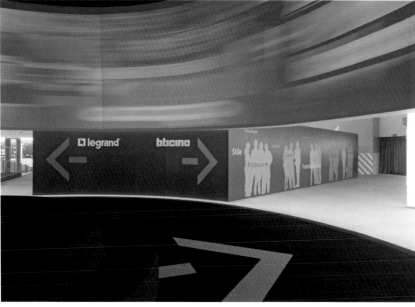

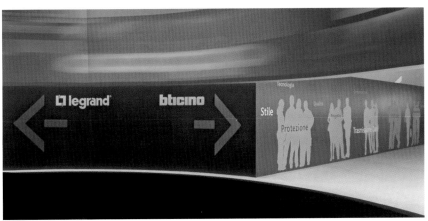

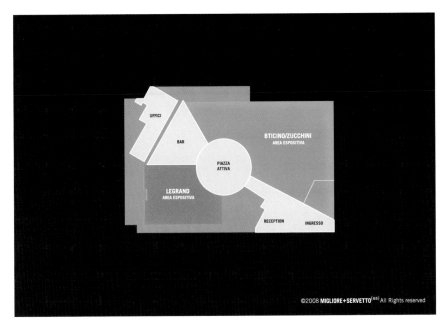

Coordination

Falke Stand at the Premium

Premium Exhibitions GmbH 2006, Berlin, Germany

German clothes company, Falke, presents itself here for the first time in the high fashion segment. On show are selected pieces of the new Urban Outdoor Collection. Fashion by Falke has an unmistakable functional and elegant character based on a consequent ergonomic fitting of the clothing to the human body. The idea was to try to convey the company's design philosophy through the design of their booth.

Coordination has created an environment which adapts unconditionally to the respective use and encloses the collections in a smooth flowing motion. The result is a unique and unmistakable design with a strong identity, whose minimalism transmits the desired impression of luxury.

Central element of the space is the custom designed fair counter "Wingboard", which takes on all communicative functions and gives direction and orientation to the space. This striking counter is echoed across the wall of the stand by way of a white stripe, which continues on the floor. These two features form a sharp and eye-catching contrast to the gloss black back wall. Falke's mannequins display the clothing on the right-hand side of the booth while the items hang from metal bars on the left.

The walls and platforms are constructed from melamine laminated MDF boards with a piano lacquer finish. This is contrasted by the gray rubber granulate floor with embedded sparkles, giving the booth an exclusive yet sporty overall appearance.

Design:
Coordination Ausstellungs GmbH
Photographs:
diephotodesigner.de
Job:
Idea, Design, Planning and Execution
Area:
105 sqm

Central element of the space is the custom designed fair counter "Wingboard", which takes on all communicative functions and gives direction and orientation to the space. This striking counter is echoed across the wall of the stand by way of a white stripe, which continues on the floor. These two features form a sharp and eye-catching contrast to the gloss black back wall. Falke's mannequins display the clothing on the right-hand side of the booth while the items hang from metal bars on the left.

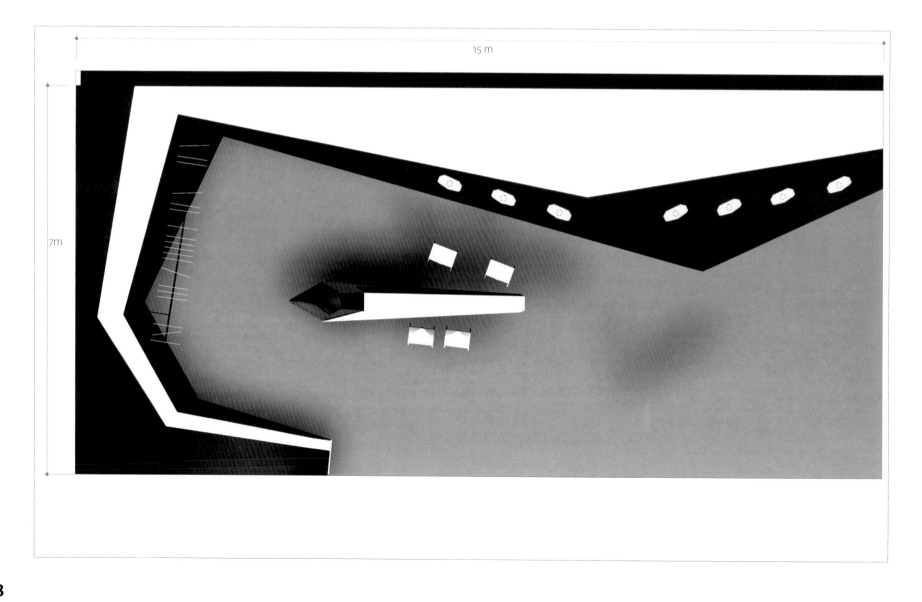

Estudio SPACETHINKING

Alumafel

Veteco 2006, Madrid, Spain

This project responds to the slogan "Neuronal Forest" and won first prize at the Stands Competition at Veteco 2006. Commissioned by ALUMAFEL, it develops from a fragmented aluminum epidermis, which in turn generates a visually and programmatically permeable membrane. This membrane defines an interior space, which is entirely linked to the exterior but, at the same time, generates a clearly defined and delineated exhibition space.

The architects define the "Neuronal Forest" as the materialization of a boundary, created from a metamorphosing warp. Its lines unfold, breaking and changing in scale, throughout the envelope of the exhibition space.

Three spatial identities appear: the first, the exterior identity, generated from the permeable envelope, which acts as a visual filter; the second, the edge identity, generated by the boundaries, which acquire their own architectural presence. Images appear in the interior of this 50 cm thick skin that reflect the shortening of the branches that emerge around it due to the angle of vision. Finally there is the interior identity, understood as "the gift", once the outer wrapping has been penetrated.

In the first of these "identities" defined by the architects, the neuronal stalks which emerge from the horizontal platform and extend along the surface perimeter define an aluminum with its own character. It is both warm and organic, because of the geometry of its forms, and crystalline and geometric, thanks to the essence of this material. This geometry, characterized by the broken and differently sized lines of aluminum, creates a strikingly bold stage.

In the interior another metamorphosis takes place as the light becomes a frame, which outlines the silhouettes of the aluminum. This process of artificial photosynthesis – understood as light that transmutes into metallic material – strengthens the magical interior of the metal box. The frames on the walls are enhanced and become the element that conceptually defines a curtain wall without glass, the material which ordinarily would characterize it and give it form.

The architects abstract the essence of a vacuum, dematerializing the façade, which is transformed into a kind of "trapped air". The curtain-wall-without-curtain mutates and becomes a boundary defined by the air between the elements, which characterize and define the "Neuronal Forest".

Design:
Studio Spacethinking: Esther Jiménez Herráiz , Jorge Tacone
Photographs:
Carlos Pesqueira & Alfonso Herranz
Builder:
ATRIUM
Area:
363,48 sqm

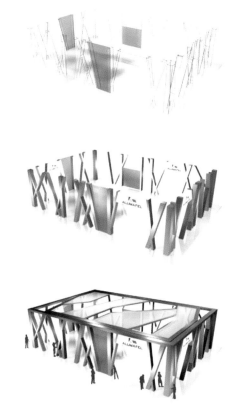

Bonjoch associats

Elisava

Student trade fair 2007, Barcelona, Spain

The stand occupied an L-shaped space and was located in a corner of the tradefair pavilion. With a surface area of just 55 sqm (590 sqft) it attempted to attract the attention of a young public who came to the fair to find out about universities and other educational possibilities.

The design of this stand, created by Ignasi Bonjoch, was based on three backlit red arches, which enclosed this distinctive space. These were complemented by the promotional phrase: "I'm not an artist" as a paradigm of design school Elisava's academic leanings. The silhouettes of visitors and staff stood out against the light, like black and white illustrations or ink drawings.

The stand's corner location meant visitors had to approach the stand from one of the two ends, perceiving the front arch as a straight wall. Only at a closer distance was it possible to see the curve of the upper section, at which point the central arch appeared as a straight wall. This was due to the arrangement of the three arches at 45 and 90 degree angles.

The public were attended, mainly by Elisava students, on round tables surrounded by red Panton de Vitra chairs. As an annex, three poufs, also in red, offered visitors a more informal setting in which to speak with the staff. The combination of volumes, colors and backlighting was lightly reflected in the white, stratified flooring.

Design:
Ignasi Bonjoch.

Photography:
Eloi Bonjoch

Technicians:
Montaggio

Area:
55 sqm

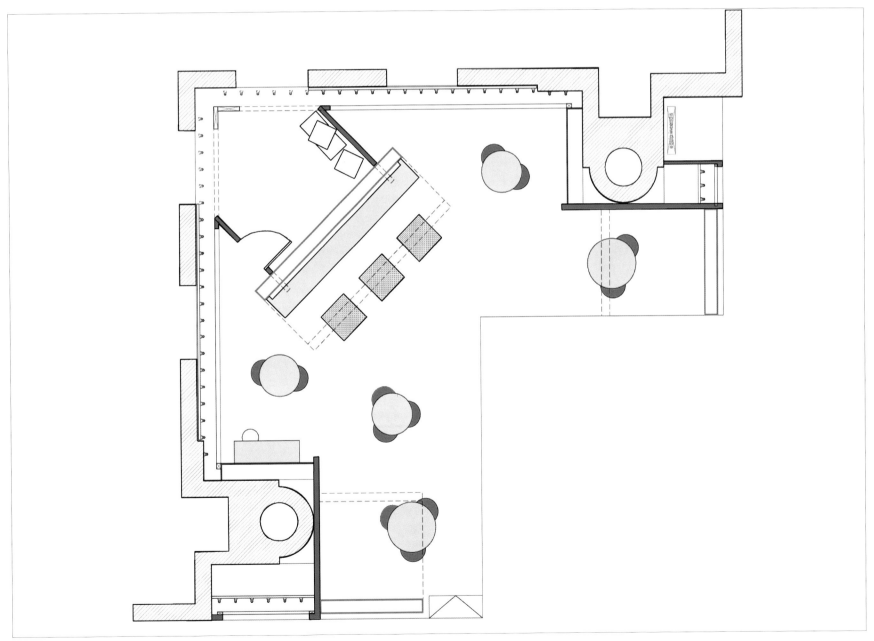

Graduat Superior en Disseny

Enginyeria Tècnica en Disseny Industrial

Arquitectura Tècnica

Màsters i Postgraus

Cicles Formatius en Disseny

↘
www.elisava.net

ELISAVA
Escola Superior de Disseny

Centre adscrit a la

UNIVERSITAT
POMPEU FABRA

The public were attended, mainly by Elisava students, on round tables surrounded by red Panton de Vitra chairs. As an annex, three poufs, also in red, offered visitors a more informal setting in which to speak with the staff. The combination of volumes, colors and backlighting was lightly reflected in the white, stratified flooring.

Jorge Hernández de la Garza

Comex

Expo Cihac 2007, Mexico

Expo –Cihac 2007 is one of the most important events in the construction industry. For Comex, a world leader in paints and coatings, it was their platform for displaying their products. Their temporary pavilion combined the company's technology, their avant-garde outlook, and their leadership within the market.

The Comex 2007 pavilion is based on a large sculptural object, which is molded by way of perforations and inclined soffits and walls. A uniform structure has been created that rises from its base on a series of columns dividing and delineating spaces and activities. All of these are connected to one another and help to offer the visitor a unique experience.

Technology is present throughout the pavilion. Thanks to a lighting system the interior transforms into different shades, which change over time and modify the perception of the pavilion. Likewise, a large wall with plasma screens in the center area shows the company's corporate videos, as well as live transmissions from the catwalk displaying the color range that Comex offers.

The interior is colorfully decorated with photographs, which lend emphasis to Comex's range of paints. Below them are color samples such as you might see in a paint shop.

Design:
Jorge Hernandez de la Garza

Photographs:
Paul Czitrom

Collaborators:
Javier Pichardo
Paula Campos
Rodrigo Ambriz

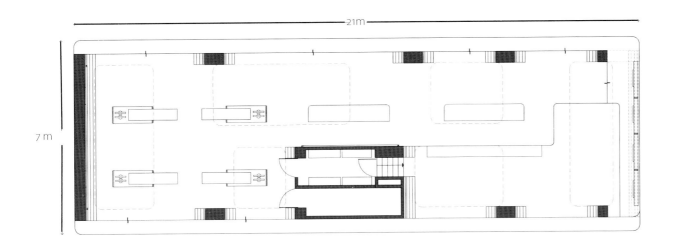

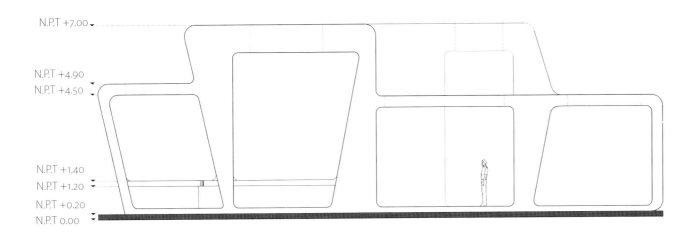

N.P.T +7.00

N.P.T +4.90
N.P.T +4.50

N.P.T +1.40
N.P.T +1.20

N.P.T +0.20
N.P.T 0.00

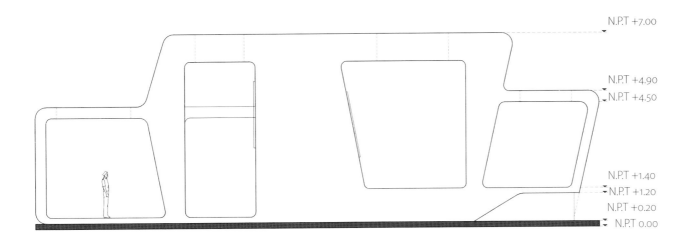

N.P.T +7.00

N.P.T +4.90
N.P.T +4.50

N.P.T +1.40
N.P.T +1.20
N.P.T +0.20
N.P.T 0.00

Walbert-Schmitz

Wolf Garten

GAFA 2006, Cologne, Germany

Internationally renowned garden tool manufacturer, Wolf Garten presented itself at the International Garden Trade Fair, GAFA 2006, as an innovative, international market leader in the garden market.

The red and yellow color combination used for the brand image was utilized to demonstrate strength. The company commissioned the designers to create an atmosphere in which the visitors could relax and experience the product world of Wolf Garten. They wanted to transmit the notion that garden work should no longer be perceived as being an annoying obligation, but through the use of Wolf Garten products, can be developed into a passion. In addition, the idea was to create a space solution by using an impressive stand architecture following the dynamic, linear style of the Wolf Garten product range.

The interior of the stand presented the garden as an extension of the living room. Subsequently, the terrace-shaped communication area, served as a platform for the grass-cutting product presentation. These products were displayed on surfaces at different heights, which appropriately resembled grass. The 6 m (20 ft) high, red external walls were intended to symbolize scale and strength and at the same time attracted the desired attention to the hall.

Inside the exhibition booth the visitor was immersed into the world of Wolf Garten. The corporate colors red and yellow were applied throughout, forming striking contrasts with more natural colors and materials. A combination of trees and bushes created an environment reminiscent of a garden, which enticed visitors to stay. The stand was also interactive, since visitors could try out garden tools and examine lawn mowers. They also had the opportunity to experience the quality of the company's range of lawn seeds, in an area aptly dubbed the petting zoo.From the lounge visitors were treated to views over the 'garden' from the balcony, which created a relaxing, homely atmosphere. This viewpoint offered a general image of the products on display as well as allowing people to take in the striking colors from the brand image.

Design:
Walbert-Schmitz

Photographs:
contributed by Walbert-Schmitz

Concept:
James T. Dickerson for Walbert Schmitz

Area:
1300 sqm

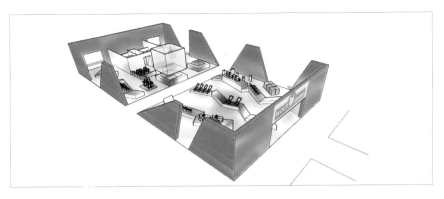

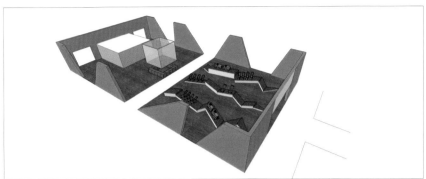

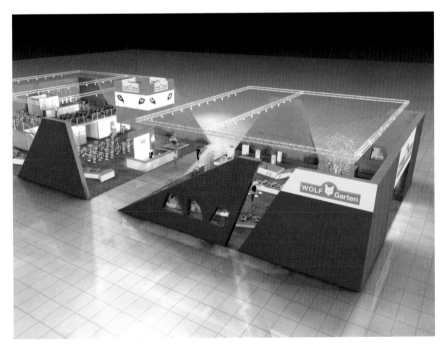

The 6 m high, red external walls are intended to symbolize scale and strength and obtained at the same time the desired attention in the hall. Inside the exhibition booth the visitor was immersed into the Wolf Garten world.

The corporate colors red and yellow were largely applied, where natural colors and materials offered the necessary contrast. In combination with trees and bushes a garden atmosphere was created, which invited to linger.

häfelinger + wagner design
Munksjö Decor

Interzum 2007, Cologne, Germany

Every other year, Interzum, an international trade fair of the furniture supplier industry, takes place in Cologne. Munksjö Decor – one of the world's leading suppliers of decorative paper for the wood and timber-processing industry – once again had häfelinger + wagner create the concept and execution of its design for the 2007 tradeshow.

Following the motto of 'Value! Created by Munksjö', the exhibition constituted the highlight event of the promotion campaign for the repositioning of Munksjö Decor. The repositioning aimed at reinforcing the company's claim of offering premium products and to demonstrate the value added of Munkjö Decor premium products with the slogan 'The Value-Added Company'. Transforming paper into space and demonstrating the creative dimensions of Munksjö decorative paper through shapes and spaces not seen before – these were the ideas that were expressed in the briefing. The concept translates the freedom gained by the reorganization of the company through a 'paper sculpture' rising from the floor. The ribbon-like paper rises and falls, sinuously flowing around one corner of the booth and displaying the company's slogans on its underside. Technical competence, innovation and a corporate message are all transferred into a spatial dimension.

The entire architecture of the exhibition stand – facades, tables and bar – quotes the architectonic execution of the sculpture. An object thus turns into a coherent communicative space of experience. The floor that has been uncovered where the paper has broken through reveals the company's main color – red – and features Munksjö Decor as a creative initiator of decorative paper innovations.

Design:
häfelinger + wagner design
Photographs:
contributed by häfelinger + wagner design
Area:
255 sqm

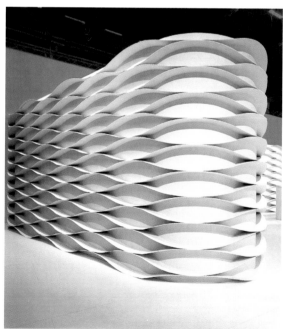

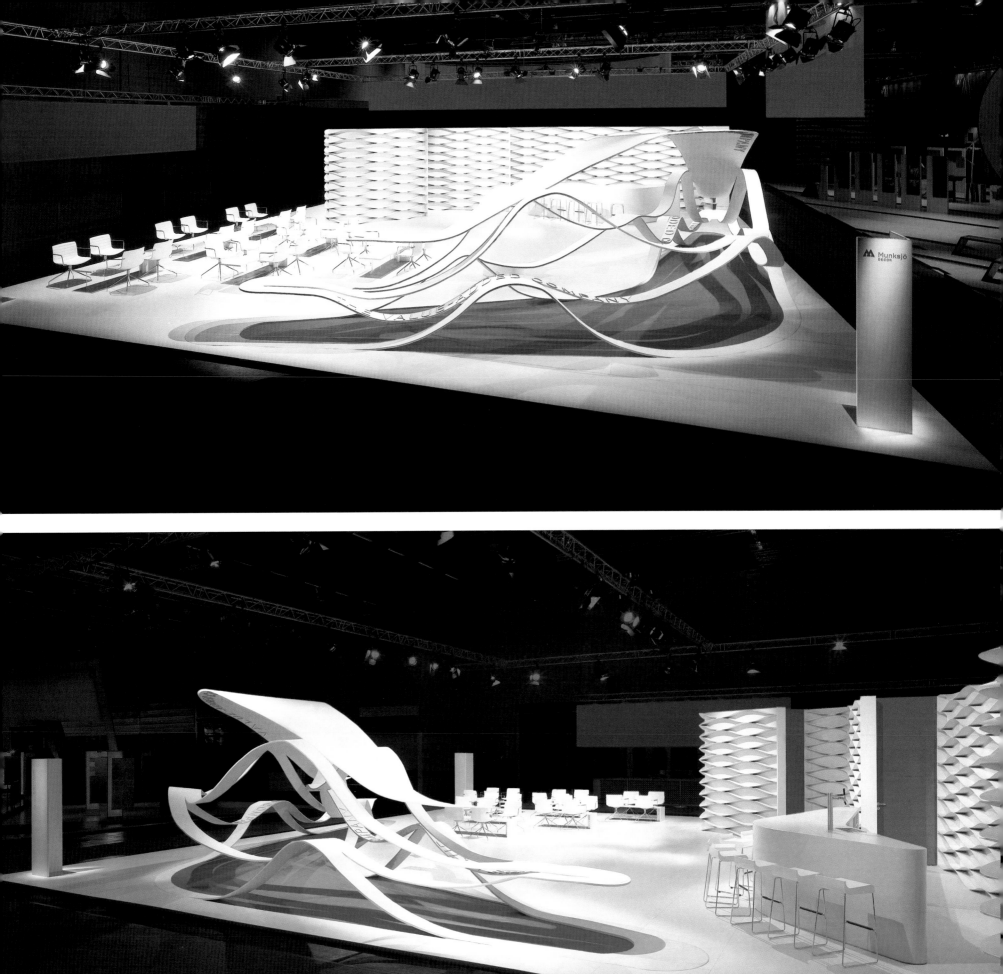

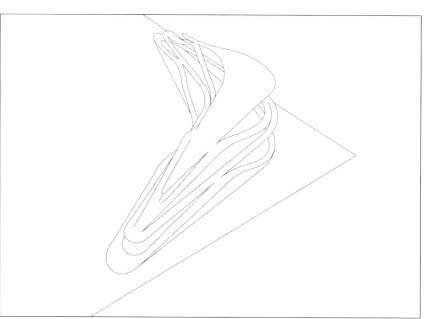

Vicente Arroyo & Isabel Colino

Nemetschek

Construtec 2006, Madrid, Spain

The aim of the "Stand Designs, Construtec 2006" contest (promoted by the COAM[1]) was to design stands while taking advantage of the product potential of participating companies.

Nemetschek is a software company whose products are immaterial. To express this immaterialness, the architects chose large bright surfaces for the floor and roof which, when lit, would generate a volume of light. They pierced this volume by "switching off" areas, thus creating the various zones where the different stand activities took place. For this, the geometry of the circumference was covered so that it facilitated a meeting space for mingling and communicating. Each circle held a specific activity—one space for each activity, without breaking the stand's continuity. The circles mingled inviting guests to pass from one to the other on its tangencies and were cut against the exterior parallelepiped revealing their interior activity in a veiled manner.

It was constructed with light. The space, defined by the beams of light, materialised with silver plated aluminium chains, with a brilliant surface and varying degrees of transparency that stir incidental reflections of light, further increasing the space's definition. The chosen material created the necessary physical boundary on the edges of the stand without losing its transparency. The resulting pavilion was penetrable in its entire perimeter like a nebula with a certain mysterious halo that invites the visitor to discover its interior. Once inside, the flexibility and permeability could be noted from the different areas; however they held the necessary independence to develop the different product presentation activities. Inside, crossing the mass of light to pass from one space to another was an entertaining experience that livened up the visit and will stay in the memory of the visitor. Some of the chains changed to a darker colour on the facades drawing the logo and the slogans of the company. The client company's corporate colours were used throughout the stand.

In these types of projects, one should work keeping themes in mind like spatial flexibility, standardization and prefabrication that permit a clean and quick stand setup, as well as consider its relocation to other fairs, since this type of setup means saving time and money. In this case they worked with the minimals; building the stand with the use of only one material, aluminium curtains that came from the factory mounted on tracks, each one in its own numbered box according to the graphic documents, which permitted that the stand was able to be set up in two hours. To find the material that would complete these requirements—above the desired transparency, permeability, colour, shine and reflection—was the largest goal in the development of the project.

The contest jury valued the capacity to generate an ambiguous enclosure that would permit combining the intense internal activities of the company with visibility from the outside.

The participating companies looked for the creation of an innovative image capable of contributing a new character to the classic stand concept. The architects' proposal always had the intention of strengthening attraction toward the exhibited product and pursued not only creating a space, but a fun and recreational experience that would encourage a visit, staying in the memory of the guest who would have seen and visited dozens of other stands at the fair.

Design:
Vicente Arroyo and Isabel Colino, architects
Photographs:
contributed by Vicente Arroyo and Isabel Colino

The space, defined by the beams of light, materialised with silver plated aluminium chains, with a brilliant surface and varying degrees of transparency that stir incidental reflections of light, further increasing the space's definition. The chosen material created the necessary physical boundary on the edges of the stand without losing its transparency. The resulting pavilion was penetrable in its entire perimeter like a nebula with a certain mysterious halo that invites the visitor to discover its interior.

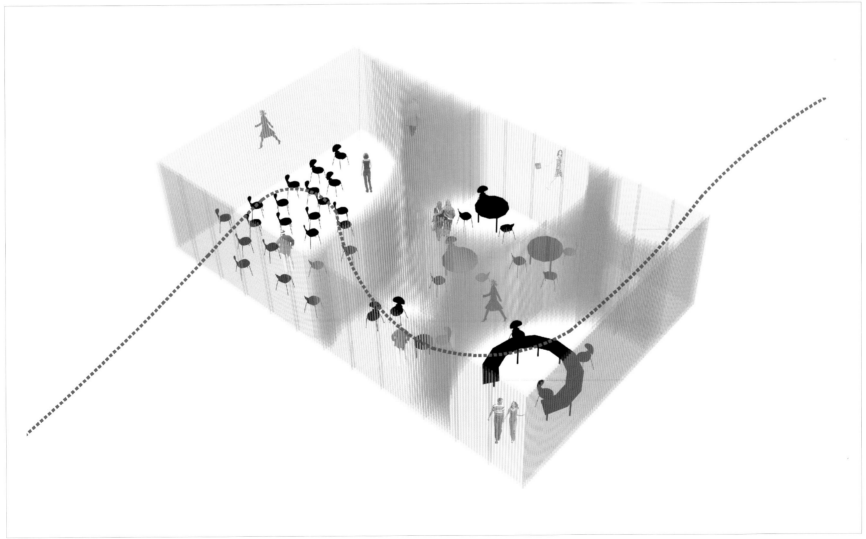

Once inside, the flexibility and permeability could be noted from the different areas; however they held the necessary independence to develop the different product presentation activities. Inside, crossing the mass of light to pass from one space to another was an entertaining experience that livened up the visit and will stay in the memory of the visitor.

Quinze & Milan

DreamSaver

Swarovksi Crystal Palace exhibition 2007, Milan, Italy

Once again design team Quinze & Milan have come up with a structure that draws visitors in, enticed by the possibility of becoming a part of the art and being effected by it. This installation was designed for Milan's Swaroski Crystal Palace, a revolutionary concept aimed at reinventing and revitalizing the chandelier. The event organizers invited eighteen leading designers to create their own contemporary interpretation of the chandelier, to give new expression to its story, meaning and message. Quinze & Milan's efforts came in the shape of DreamSaver.

According to Arne Quinze: 'When walking through the DreamSaver one experiences the magic of crystals: they preserve the dreams and energy of the people who passed through it before you. Interactive and enchanting, DreamSaver is a prototype for an energy transmission craft in which each visitor exudes and absorbs energy. Sounds whisper in your ear. Changing colors bedazzle the senses. Its looks are shaped by motion: it freezes the moment without losing speed.'

Inspiration for DreamSaver came from Arne Quinze's desire to revert the experience of looking at crystals from the outside and using them as a source of reflection. Quinze's aim is to use the emotional capacity of Swarovski crystal to absorb and release the energy and dreams of people. By doing so, the crystals "look" at the viewer and become a form of energy by turn. Shaped for speed and motion, when walking through DreamSaver, visitors experience the magic of the crystals and at the same time feel the energy of the previous visitors.

The structure is a 12m (40 ft) long and 3m (10ft) high tunnel and has been made using a wooden and metal frame coated in eight layers of multi-structured fiberglass sheets coated in a Ceralic metallic lacquer. Inside, there are six projection units and hanging from it are 5.5km (3.4 miles) of Swarovski crystal strands.

Design & concept:
Arne Quinze

Photographs:
Thierry van Dort for Quinze & Milan

Construction:
Quinze & Milan

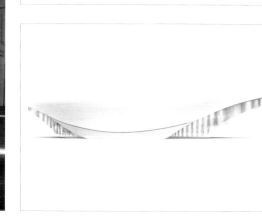

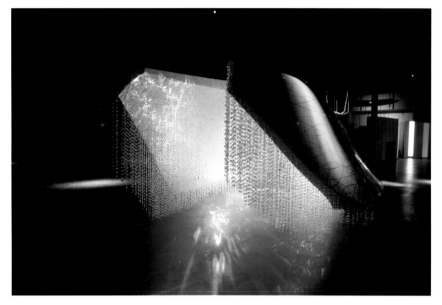

Quinze's aim is to use the emotional capacity of Swarovski crystal to absorb and release the energy and dreams of people. By doing so, the crystals "look" at the viewer and become a form of energy by turn. Shaped for speed and motion, when walking through Dream Saver, visitors experience the magic of the crystals and at the same time feel the energy of the previous visitors.

The structure is a 12m (40 ft) long and 3m (10ft) high tunnel and has been made using a wooden and metal frame coated in eight layers of multi-structured fiberglass sheets coated in a Ceralic metallic lacquer. Inside, there are six projection units and hanging from it are 5.5km (3.4 miles) of Swarovski crystal strands.

Estudio SPACETHINKING

Akaba

OFITEC 2006, Madrid, Spain

This ephemeral architecture won first prize in the COAM competition (Official Architects' Association of Madrid) in association with IFEMA (Trade Fair Institution of Madrid) as a stand for OFITEC 2006 with the slogan "Wide Curtain".

The architects responsible for the project understood that a stand proposal goes beyond just a description of the product. This is why they designed and produced this stand using Akaba's new company philosophy, "Akaba: New Experiences", as a guiding principle. The final result surprised visitors to the OFITEC trade fair and encouraged them to reflect. The stand consisted in the construction of a "company lattice" made from the exhibition object itself, which defined the boundaries of the exhibition space.

The architects created a double skin (dubbed "the curtain") made from a simple metal structure, above which the new collections of chairs floated, held up by metal wires. The object was decontextualized through this subterfuge, thus acquiring a significant aesthetic and symbolic presence. The exhibition was programmed in two large core areas: the first around the singular elements (the "company lattice"), where the new collection of chairs was on display, and the second around the modular elements distributed across the exhibition floor, displaying objects from the new table collection.

Design:
Esther Jiménez Herráiz
Jorge Tacone
Photographs:
Estudio Spacethinking
Builder:
IDEAFIX
Area:
189 sqm

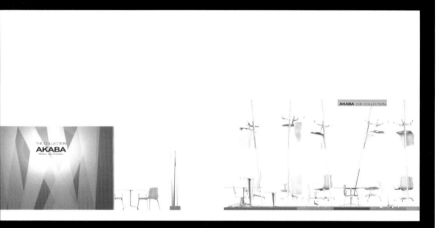

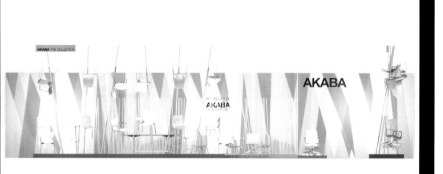

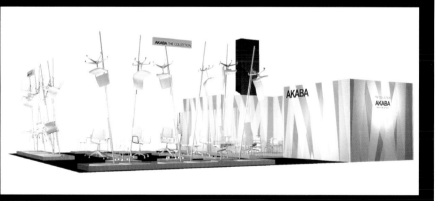

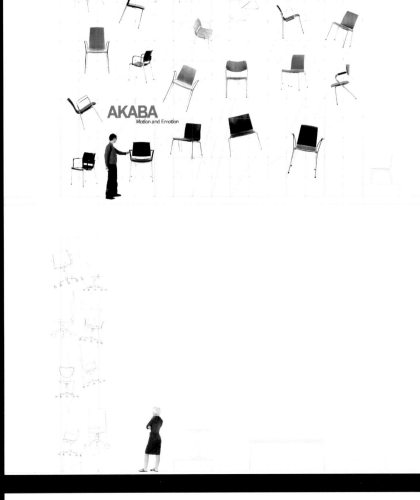

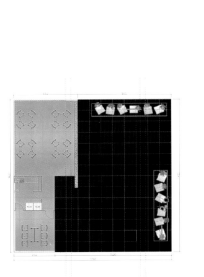

D'Art Design Gruppe

Grundig Intermedia GmbH

IFA 2007, Berlin, Germany

Grundig Intermedia GmbH strikes a very positive balance this year in its presentation at the IFA 2007. Not only has the well-known German electronics firm presented numerous innovations, but also has reached new records in sales and visitors. The objective of the presentation was to renew consumer and merchant trust in the brand and, as a result, awaken a new feeling for it.

Situated in pavilion 23b with a total exhibition of 2,200 sqm, Grundig highlights its image in consumer electronics as a quality brand that is both dynamic and modern.

The "emotional landscape" concept goes for vibrancy and dynamism, focused, doubtlessly, on the product presentation. Open spaces were created for it using architectural resources offered by the surroundings. The only elements of the "emotional landscape" that trace the closed space are a few large, white hollow tubes scattered throughout the exhibition. Thanks to the ample amount used and their distribution, a visual panorama of islands and expansive spaces is achieved, which form coordinated areas, directing the visitors from one zone to the next.

This correlation is developed from the outside in, from the firm's emblem to each one of the exclusive exhibitions of its products. The visitor is guided along surprising paths through the experimental world of Grundig, discovering, little by little, its great variety of products. The distinct areas are dynamically integrated into the emotional landscape and each display follows its own theatrics and expressions, adapting to particular characteristics and necessities of the products. Therefore each area becomes its own world. An interactive station has been installed in each one of them where the visitors can experience the technical advantages of Grundig's best. In the soundproof cabins the visitors can be taken away by great sound quality, for example, or in the portable electronics area they can experience the next generation of MP3 players.

This exhibition is directed as much to Grundig's merchants as well as to its customers. It varies from indulging those who simply come to visit, to those who like to experience the merchandise, thereby having the opportunity to try out and appreciate the new Grundig products for themselves. Thus, the exhibition is based around the user and he becomes the centre of the "emotional landscape".

The merchants' zone, which occupies half of the total presentation area, follows the same principal of an "emotional landscape", though it is integrated into a more solemn environment that radiates sobriety and value, as well as generates confidence. This atmosphere of "well-being" facilitates success for conversations and business meetings.

Design:
D'Art Design Gruppe

Photographs:
contributed by D'Art Design Gruppe

Area:
2,200 sqm (24000 sqft)

PORTABLES

PORTABLE ENTERTAINMENT

The visitor is guided along surprising paths through the experimental world of Grundig, discovering, little by little, its great variety of products. The distinct areas are dynamically integrated into the emotional landscape and each display follows its own theatrics and expressions, adapting to particular characteristics and necessities of the products.

Nacho Martí

Cesda

Study Fair 2006, Barcelona, Spain

The design of a low-cost stand for the Study Fair in Barcelona; a trade fair aimed at helping young people to choose the subjects they will study at university.

The client needed a stand that would attract young visitors and awaken their curiosity regarding the world of aviation, thus encouraging them to become future students. The stand was designed to have a friendly environment that transmits a feeling of closeness through its chromatic range, graphics and furnishings. It avoids the more technological aspects of the aeronautical world in favor of the more glamorous aesthetic of the pilots and the traveling.

A single furnishing, inspired by airport check-in desks, houses the catalogues, the meeting table and provides a space for talking to visitors. A second area, delineated by the graphics on the wall is used for more informal meetings and makes use of expressive and attractive furnishings. The long and narrow storage room acts as a canvass where the corporate image is applied. The lighting has been solved by concealing the fluorescent bulbs inside the clouds that hang from the ceiling of the pavilion.

Design:
Nacho Marti, designer
Otto & Olaf, art & communication
Photographs:
Gogortza & Llorella
Builder:
Servis Complet
Area:
40 sqm

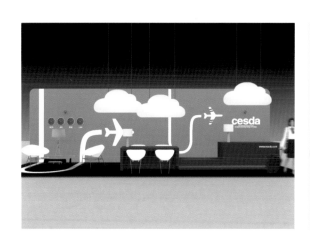
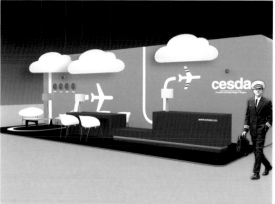

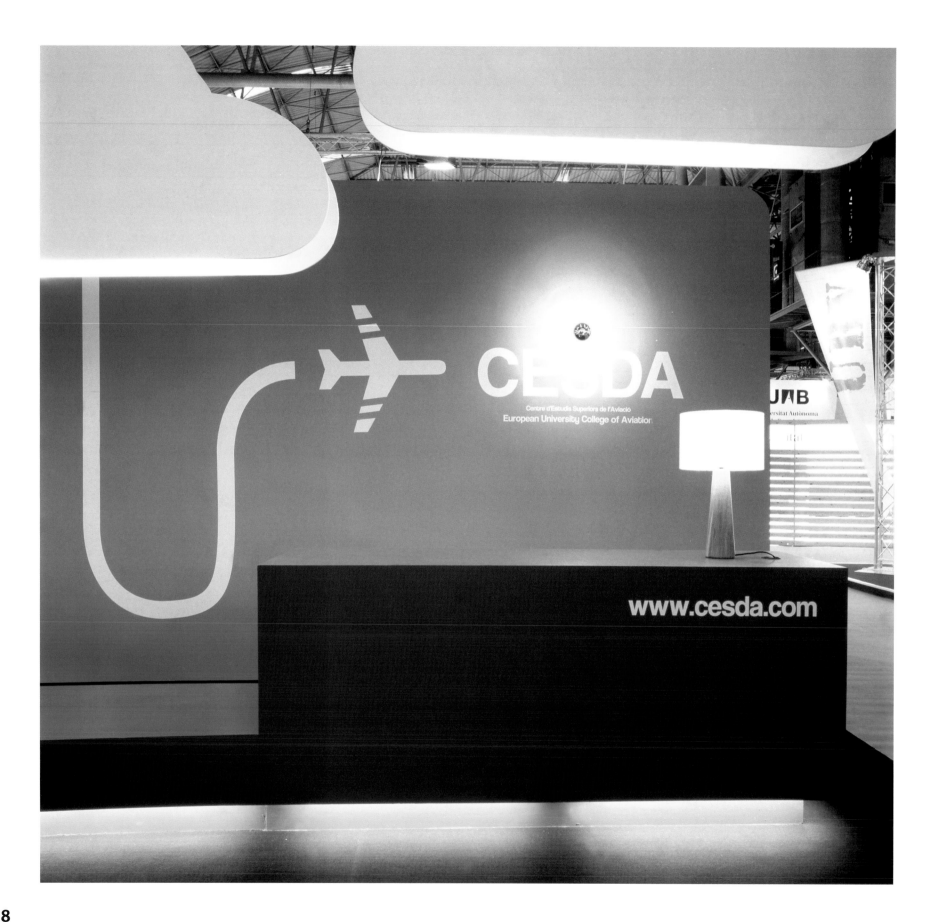

Gannaca

Skiny Bodywear

Body Look 2006, Düsseldorf, Germany

The creative brand communications, gannaca, designed a trade fair stand for the young Austrian lingerie label Skiny Under-wear at the international body wear platform BODY LOOK 2006 (CPD Düsseldorf).

Christopher Peterka, managing partner, and designer Anne-Katrin Ahrens crafted the extraordinary stand. Their dynamic, yet simple white cube was symbolically held together by blue and black tape announcing the 'Skiny Revolution'. Their artwork demonstrated an enormous expressiveness, intensity and drive.

The advertising campaign behind the concept, which showed the German actor Til Schweiger on the run following a romantic interlude, defined the core concept. The important elements: a revolving door, a balcony and a couch were integrated directly into the stand. The reappearance of his silhouette as a body in flight in each part of the stand and the use of lines of tape to trace a path through its interior symbolizes the speed and dynamics of the action. Outlines of the negative figures were illuminated indirectly by a cool white light inserted between the two layers of the double-walled structure. Altogether gannaca used 8,602 ft (800 m2) of drapery, 1,500 kg of aluminium, 0.62 miles (1 km) of cable, 0.93 miles (1.5 km) of tape and 197 yards (180 m) of neon lamps.

Skiny Bodywear made a lasting impression with gannaca's taped-up stand. Unlike other stands, not a single pair of knick-ers, a bra or a swimsuit was to be seen. Neither inside nor outside logos or glaring ads were used. When the logo is no longer the star of the show, a new area emerges within which the brand can present its image. It's all about radical reduction and maximum appeal. Coupled with the tape, the 'escape' silhouettes conveyed a message strong enough to eliminate the need for any product display at all.

Design:
Gannaca (Christopher Peterka & Anne-Katrin Arens)

Photographs:
Lionel Samain

Sketches:
Anne-Katrin Ahrens

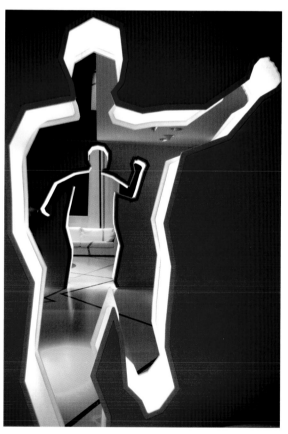

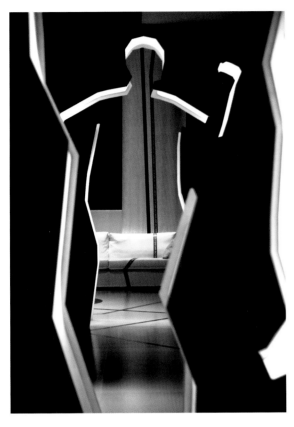
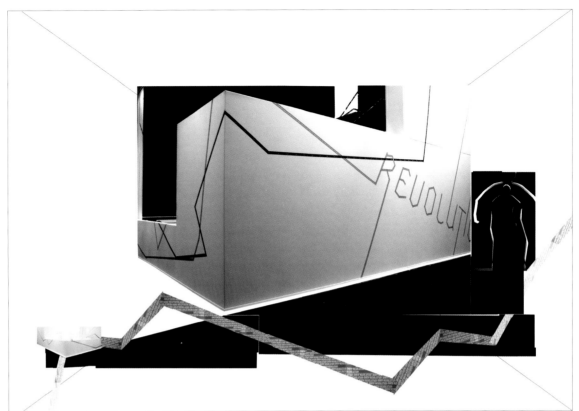

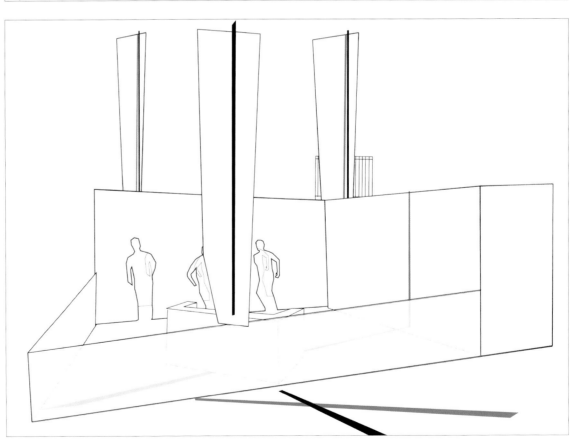

Simone Micheli

Cheap & Chic – The Hotel for our Time

Sia Guest, 2006, Rimini, Italy

At the Sia Guest Hotel Fair in Rimini for the event "Dormire Altrove", architect Simone Micheli presented cheap & chic: a project which celebrated the world of hospitality through the cross-section of a futuristic hotel. The stand included the hotel corridor, bedroom with bathroom and meeting-lounge area. The space created constituted an anti-mimetic, emotional design linked to modernity. This was a suggestive space designed for encounters, with an appearance that would fit somewhere between the present and the future of the hotel world. It constituted a visual display of a new conception of hospitality, turning to a "low-cost" dimension without negating the services and the quality of the space, enhancing the link between the personality of the setting, perceptions and functionality.

The idea behind the hotel, characterized by proportioned and contained sale prices of the room and construction costs, thanks to the exuberance of the project, the applied technology and the integrated materials, was the significant suggestion the projected space could emanate. It was the perceived value, the living in "another" space, in a contemporary work that became fundamental. The transversal idea expressed by the project consisted in imagining a hotel which consented to give life to iconic spaces, shapes and realities able to insert themselves naturally in our everyday life.

This huge suite is obviously one of total luxury. Flush lighting in the ceiling projects white spots in all different directions. This apparently chaotic design scheme is repeated on the walls and furnishings, which all have swirling patterns, inviting the guest to enter both a futuristic and somewhat psychedelic world. The chaos is offered some kind of organization through the white ceiling and floor and the restricted color scheme for the rest of the space, which alternates between black with white swirls and blue with black swirls. The fact that the scheme is repeated throughout the entire space, including the bathroom and corridor, further contributes to this uniformity. Floor to ceiling mirrors located behind the bar area offer the suite a greater sense of size. The prestigious companies that made this fascinating installation were selected by Micheli for their high quality and reliability, their use of technology, their extensive productive capability and for their entrepreneurial spirit.

Design:
Arch. Simone Micheli

Photographs:
Paolo Zitti

This huge suite is obviously one of total luxury. Flush lighting in the ceiling projects white spots in all different directions. This apparently chaotic design scheme is repeated on the walls and furnishings, which all have swirling patterns, inviting the guest to enter both a futuristic and somewhat psychedelic world. The chaos is offered some kind of organization through the white ceiling and floor and the restricted color scheme for the rest of the space, which alternates between black with white swirls and blue with black swirls.

Patricia Urquiola + Martino Berghinz

Moroso

Salone del Mobile 2007, Milan, Italy

Moroso design is global. It unites diversities. It does not seek standardisation but instead the opportunity for making different cultures and idioms interact creatively, which then grow richer by coming together and generate interesting and extraordinary projects, full of meaning and value.

The choice of an international team of designers whose origins range from northern Europe to the Mediterranean basin, from the Middle to the Far East (in pursuit of new design inputs that join different cultures and lifestyles) feeds and enriches the company's know-how which, through exchange and dialogue, is constantly renewed.

To highlight its globality, this year at Milan fair Moroso is to present many different products of great personality, the result of specific research expressed in many styles set within a space designed by Patricia Urquiola together with Martino Berghinz.

The exhibition stand is broken up geometrically by the volumes which are seen to float above the products. Thus luminous partitions are formed in which the expressions of the various designers are combined, forming new furnishing solutions. White makes the atmosphere neutral, allowing full freedom for the product colour schemes, while the shapes and volumes suggest to the public how to use the space.

Design:
Patricia Urquiola + Martino Berghinz

Photographs:
contributed by Moroso

Winntech 2004

Global Shop 2004, Las Vegas, USA

Winntech, a retail, fixture and merchandising design firm based in Kansas City, has been on the cutting edge of delivering dramatic, cost-effective, out-of-the-box solutions for their clients for well over a decade. So this stand at the 2004 Global Shop Exhibition, the world's largest annual retail design and in-store marketing trade fair, was very much in keeping with their usual style. Their mission here was to sell their creativity to merchandising companies and therefore to come up with a focal point intriguing enough to pull attendees into the booth. Winntech's design motto for GlobalShop was: "No Time. No money. Find some way to make it work." So ideally the stand had to be simple, cheap and effective.

What was most striking upon entering the Las Vegas Convention Center was the unmistakable scent of fresh oranges. Winntech chose the orange theme to assault the senses of Global Shop visitors. While visitors are accustomed to the visual stimulation of a large trade fair event like this one, they do not expect to have their sense of smell involved as well. There were 1174 oranges in total hanging from strings, which in turn were attached to a 6 m (20 ft) truss. Each orange was strung through fishing line and secured with lead weights at the bottom of each strand. They were arranged to form a floating 3.5 m (12 ft) orange circle. Four monitors positioned above the truss ran a continuous loop of Winntech's marketing message. Directly under the oranges was a floor graphic proclaiming all the areas of expertise this award-winning designer of retail environments provides its clients. This was carried out by way of a series of sentences, phrases, and words printed on the white platform. This stand fulfilled all the requisites the designers set themselves in their design motto. It took no time at all to erect, cost around 35 dollars per square foot and became one of the talking points of the trade fair.

Design:
Winntech

Photographs:
contributed by Winntech

298